Quebec 1775

The American invasion of Canada

Campaign · 128

OSPREY
PUBLISHING

Quebec 1775

The American invasion of Canada

Brendan Morrissey · Illustrated by Adam Hook

Series editor Lee Johnson · Consultant editor David G Chandler

First published in Great Britain in 2003 by Osprey Publishing, Elms Court,
Chapel Way, Botley, Oxford OX2 9LP, United Kingdom.
Email: info@ospreypublishing.com

A CIP catalogue record for this book is available from the British Library

ISBN 1 84176 681 X

Editor: Lee Johnson
Design: The Black Spot
Index by Alan Thatcher
Maps by The Map Studio
3D bird's-eye views by The Black Spot
Battlescene artwork by Adam Hook
Originated by The Electronic Page Company, Cwmbran, UK
Printed in China through World Print Ltd.

03 04 05 06 07   10 9 8 7 6 5 4 3 2 1

For a catalog of all books published by Osprey Military
and Aviation please contact:

Osprey Direct USA, c/o MBI Publishing, P.O. Box 1,
729 Prospect Ave, Osceola, WI 54020, USA
E-mail: info@ospreydirectusa.com

Osprey Direct UK, P.O. Box 140, Wellingborough,
Northants, NN8 2FA, UK
E-mail: info@ospreydirect.co.uk

www.ospreypublishing.com

Dedication

To Nora, Patrick and Emmet.

Acknowledgement

The author wishes to express his thanks to René
Chartrand, Todd Braisted at the Institute for Advanced
Loyalist Studies (www.royalprovincial.com), Kim Stacy of
the reconstructed Royal Highland Emigrants
(www.84th.com), and to Art Cohn and Brenda Hughes of
the lake Champlain Maritime museum (www.lcmm.org) for
their valuable help.

Author's Note

For brevity and continuity, the author has retained the
terminology used in his earlier titles, *Boston 1775, Saratoga
1777,* and *Yorktown 1781* (Campaign Series Nos. 37, 67,
and 47): "American" refers to the forces of Congress, and
"Loyalist" to those fighting for the King; the inhabitants of
Quebec province and Upper Canada are "Canadians"; and
the "native" peoples of North America are referred to by
their tribal names, or collectively as "Indians".
Retrospective terms such as "Native American" and
"Patriot" have been avoided. "New York" refers to the
colony/state and "New York City" to the conurbation on the
Manhattan peninsula; similarly, "Quebec" refers to the city
and "the Province of Quebec" to the colony. As always, the
author has tried to use contemporary illustrations that best
depict the people, places, and events described.

Artist's note

KEY TO MILITARY SYMBOLS

CONTENTS

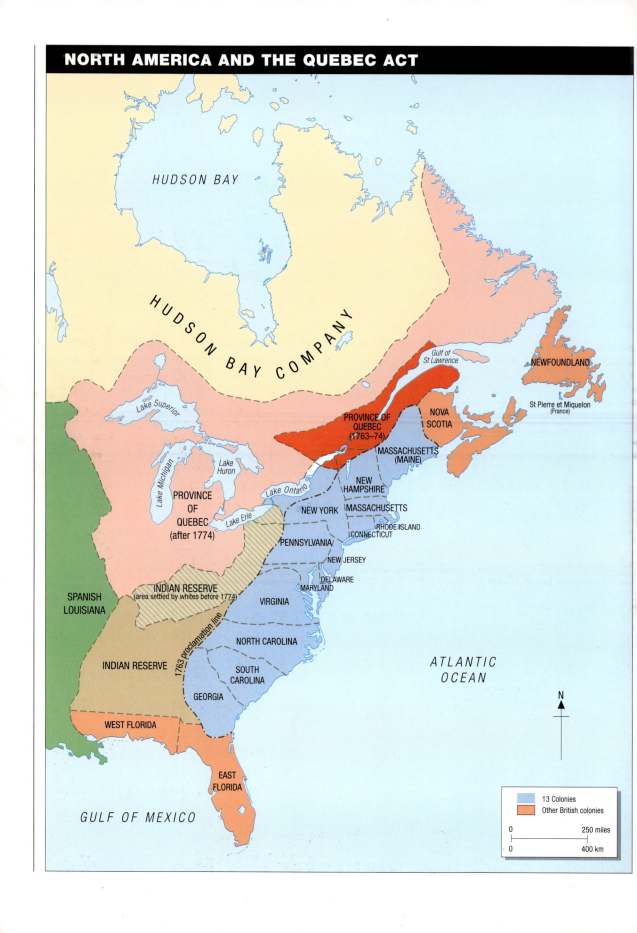

NORTH AMERICA AND THE QUEBEC ACT

HUDSON BAY

HUDSON BAY COMPANY

Lake Superior

Lake Michigan

Lake Huron

Lake Erie

Lake Ontario

Gulf of St Lawrence

NEWFOUNDLAND

St Pierre et Miquelon
(France)

PROVINCE OF
QUEBEC
(1763–74)

NOVA
SCOTIA

MASSACHUSETTS
(MAINE)

PROVINCE
OF
QUEBEC
(after 1774)

NEW
HAMPSHIRE

NEW YORK

MASSACHUSETTS

RHODE ISLAND
CONNECTICUT

PENNSYLVANIA

NEW JERSEY

DELAWARE
MARYLAND

INDIAN RESERVE
(area settled by whites before 1774)

SPANISH
LOUISIANA

VIRGINIA

1763 proclamation line

INDIAN RESERVE

NORTH CAROLINA

SOUTH
CAROLINA

GEORGIA

ATLANTIC
OCEAN

N

WEST FLORIDA

EAST
FLORIDA

GULF OF MEXICO

13 Colonies
Other British colonies

0   250 miles
0   400 km

THE ROAD TO QUEBEC

INTRODUCTION

The invasion of Canada (or more accurately the Province of Quebec) by the forces of Congress is one of the strangest incidents in an unusual conflict. It was a campaign littered with paradoxes, including French-speaking Catholics fighting for a Protestant Great Britain, one army besieging another almost three times its size, and strategic failure resulting from tactical success.

The Treaty of Paris, in 1763, had ended 150 years of French rule north and east of the Great Lakes and west of the Allegheny Mountains. While the Illinois and Ohio country remained untamed, within the Province of Quebec, direct and absolute rule from Versailles gave way to more liberal government from London, which soon elicited a similar view of individual liberty and independence as that found among Great Britain's other North American colonies. It was this perceived empathy – and the strategic implications of the British military presence to the north – that prompted Congress to consider "liberating" Canada.

Death of Montgomery, by J. Trumbull. Trumbull's works are often just a collection of portraits in a historical setting, but here he has attempted to depict an actual event, with accurate uniforms and numbers of participants. (Anne S.K. Brown Military Collection)

CANADA AND THE THIRTEEN COLONIES

Having spent considerable sums of money – and blood – defending its North American colonies from the French and their Indian allies, Great Britain felt justified in asking for some measure of repayment from the colonists. Powerful though the issue of taxation was, it merely brought to a head a much deeper division that had existed almost from the foundation of the colonies by people fleeing religious, political or social restrictions in Europe. And when the French departed, so too did the only reason for reliance on Great Britain – defense.

Against this background of political unrest, rumors circulated throughout North America of a Bill that would recognize the alien nature of the former New France. Canadians wanted their language, laws and religion recognized, and access to civil and military posts in their own country. The first two British governors – Major-General James Murray, and Major-General Guy Carleton – believed that the future of Quebec as a British colony had to be based on tolerance, and lobbied London accordingly. The only opposition came from a small but vociferous group of English-speaking immigrants, who had assumed that they would be given preference over the defeated Papists.

In 1774, Parliament passed the Quebec Act, which accepted the Catholic religion (modifying the oath, so that Catholics could hold public office), and confirmed the use of French law and custom. It also redrew the boundaries of the Province, effectively ending any westward expansion by the American colonies – particularly New York, Pennsylvania and Virginia – and lucrative land speculation by men like George Washington, Patrick Henry, and Israel Putnam. Despite being probably the most farsighted piece of legislation enacted by a British government in North America, it was widely attacked by Americans – by now paranoid about their own "liberty" – who saw no irony in denying majority rule to the Canadians.

The First Continental Congress saw Canadians as potential allies, but was also aware of their hostility toward Americans. It determined to extend the hand of friendship (the Province's commercial and agricultural assets were no doubt also a factor) and in a long-winded letter agreed on 26 October 1774, invited Canadians to put aside religious differences

Ethan Allen captures Fort Ticonderoga, artist unidentified. Allen confronts Delaplace (in this case with breeches) and claims Ticonderoga "in the name of the Great Jehovah and the Continental Congress" – a verbal flourish almost certainly added later, since eyewitnesses say he challenged the "damn'd old rat" to come out! Allen apparently wore yellow breeches and a green jacket with gold epaulettes and his account of the assault makes no mention of Arnold. When the Green Mountain Boys were re-raised in 1776, the rank-and-file voted to replace Allen with his cousin, Seth Warner, a former Rogers Ranger. (Anne S K Brown Military Collection)

and establish "a hearty amity." The letter also carried a threat, reminding Canadians they were "a small people compared to those who with open arms invite you into fellowship." At the same time, John Jay, with the knowledge of Congress, was circulating a pamphlet in North America and Great Britain alleging that the King was organizing a Canadian Catholic army to lay waste the colonies and possibly even Great Britain and Ireland as well.

The Massachusetts Committee of Correspondence dispatched an agent, John Brown, to invite American merchants in Montreal and Quebec to send delegates to Philadelphia and join in plans for rebellion. On his way, Brown looked in at Fort Ticonderoga, the former French strongpoint at the junction of Lake Champlain and Lake George that guarded the main trade route from New York and New England into Canada. He advised his masters that the post "must be seissed [sic] as soon as possible should hostilities be committed by the King's troops," and recommended a local group of vigilantes known as the Green Mountain Boys for the task.

WAR BREAKS OUT

Since the beginning of 1775, the commander at Ticonderoga, Captain William Delaplace of the 26th Foot, had been reporting suspicious activity around the post to Lieutenant-General Thomas Gage, the British commander in chief in North America. As the situation worsened, Gage warned Delaplace that a surprise attack might be imminent, although how Delaplace could have made the run-down post more secure with just two officers, 46 enlisted men (mostly old and worn out), and 24 wives and children, is unclear.

On 19 April 1775, after several near misses, hostilities did indeed break out between the King's troops and local militia, resulting in bloodshed at Lexington, Concord, and all the way back to Boston. The following day, an unofficial "army" of 20,000 militia had surrounded Boston, with more on the way – among them one Benedict Arnold. Arriving at Cambridge, Arnold persuaded the Massachusetts Provincial Congress to commission him as a colonel and authorize him to raise 500 troops to attack Ticonderoga. Leaving the mundane task of recruiting to others, he hastened north.

Ethan Allen, commander of the Green Mountain Boys, had been equally excited by the events at Boston and also decided to attack Ticonderoga. On 7 May he gathered 200 men at Castleton and arranged for boats to be brought to Hands Cove, just across the lake from the fort. As he was leaving Castleton, Arnold arrived and showed Allen his Massachusetts commission; Allen (or rather his men) refused to acknowledge it and, with the worst possible grace, the two agreed to march on the fort together. On the night of 9 May they arrived at Hands Cove, but the crossing was a shambles: only two boats could be found, and it was almost 3.00am before 83 men – all that could be carried at one time – crossed to the west side of the lake. Surprising a dozing sentry, whose musket misfired, Allen and his troops surged into the fort. Captain Delaplace and his colleague, Lieutenant Jocelyn Feltham, were roused unceremoniously from their quarters, and herded onto the

A view of Ticonderoga ("the place where the lake shuts itself") – or alternatively Cheonderoga ("brawling waters") – looking east from Mount Hope. The fort and the "French Lines" are visible in the middle ground at left. In the background are the Green Mountains of Vermont, then the New Hampshire Grants, from which Allen's unit took its name. (Author's photograph)

parade ground with their men, whereupon Allen's troops found the rum store and proceeded to get drunk.

As more Green Mountain Boys crossed the lake, Allen sent a detachment of 100 men, under Seth Warner and Remember Baker (cousin to both men), to seize Crown Point. The sergeant and ten men living there were merely glorified caretakers and put up no resistance. At the same time, 30 more men under Captain Samuel Herrick were marching to Skenesboro (now Whitehall), the seat of a prominent Loyalist, Philip Skene. Herrick found Skene's schooner, *Katherine*,[1] renamed it **Liberty** and delivered it to Ticonderoga on 14 May.

Meanwhile, Arnold had learned that the British post at St Johns, at the head of the lake, was not only unguarded, but was also home to a 16-gun sloop packed with stores. Aware that such a mission would violate the New York–Quebec frontier, and that a column of Regulars was coming from Montreal to reinforce the garrison, Arnold took over **Liberty**, and set off up Lake Champlain. Soon after dawn on 17 May, he captured the fort, its 14-man garrison, and the sloop *George III* (which he renamed **Enterprise**), destroyed some boats and stores, and returned south. On the way, he met Allen and 100 of his men, who had rowed up the lake in two bateaux.

Crown Point on Lake Champlain. Crown Point, ten miles (16km) north of Fort Ticonderoga, was fortified first by the French in 1731, and then more extensively by the British in 1759. Like Fort Ticonderoga, this post – together with Chimney Point on the opposite shore – defended another bottleneck that could hold up an enemy advancing from the south, but was very vulnerable to attack from the north. Although the works were thoroughly dilapidated by 1775, the site was used as a supply depot for the invasion of Canada, and a hospital and rallying point during the retreat. (Author's photograph)

Against Arnold's advice, Allen intended to occupy the fort and ambush the relief column coming from Chambly. He later thought better of it and withdrew to the opposite side of the river; the next morning he awoke to find 200 Regulars and two small cannon facing him from the west bank. He put his men back into the boats and had soon rowed out of range, but only after losing three men.

By the end of May, Massachusetts and Connecticut had agreed that the latter would look after the defense of the Lake Champlain corridor. Unfortunately, nobody told Arnold and on learning that his Massachusetts commission was now defunct, he took *Liberty* and *Enterprise* out into the middle of the lake. When a committee rowed out to reason with him, his crew fixed bayonets and prevented them coming aboard. Finally, they persuaded Arnold to give up the vessels, but this was just the first of a number of clashes between Arnold and his political and military masters.

---

1 British ships appear in *italics*; the names of American ships appear in *bold italics*.

THE SEAT OF WAR

GEOGRAPHY

There were three main conurbations in 18th-century Canada: Quebec, Trois Rivières, and Montreal, each surrounded by a few relatively large villages and many smaller, extended rural communities. The latter comprised long, thin farms fronting either side of a road or river, with a few non-agricultural buildings (usually a school, a parsonage, an *auberge* (inn) and tradesmen's homes) and the parish church.

These communities were surrounded by virgin forests teeming with game, similar to those in upper New York. Most of the valleys encompassing the St Lawrence River and Richelieu River were extremely flat, except for some isolated mountains at Chambly and Montreal (hence the later description of this region as "Lower Canada"). There were few roads, and those poorly maintained. However, few villages were far from a river, so water was the most common means of transport. Canadians generally used canoes hollowed out of red elm, holding up to 20 men, while Indians used birch bark smeared with pitch, around hickory frames, able to carry from two to 30 passengers.

The main waterway was the St Lawrence, which linked Quebec, Trois Rivières, and Montreal, although from 1735 they were also linked by the "Chemin du Roi" that ran parallel with, and mostly in sight of, the river. Movement of goods and people from west to east (i.e. downstream) was much faster by water than by road, but moving from east to west was more problematic. The St Lawrence was tidal only as far as Trois Rivières, beyond which it passed through Lac St Pierre and then narrowed considerably before reaching Montreal. This produced a much faster current (about 10mph compared with four between Trois Rivières and Quebec), which, with the added complication of islands and rapids just east of Montreal, made navigation hazardous. It took a skilled pilot to land a vessel at the

Passage of troops down the St Lawrence, by Thomas Davies c.1760. Painted by an eyewitness, the scene is from the French and Indian War, but illustrates perfectly the problems of transporting troops by water and the nature of the densely forested Canadian wilderness. (National Archives of Canada – C-000577)

Le Chevalier Charles Louis Tarieu de La Naudière left for France at the end of the Fench Indian War, but returned to Canada. On the outbreak of war he was one of the noblemen given a commission in the militia. (Private Collection)

St Luc de La Corne was La Naudière's father-in-law and one of the *seigneurs* who worked closely with the Indians. Initially eager to serve Carleton, he soon offered the advancing Americans an "accommodation". He eventually threw in his lot with the British and later led the Indian forces that accompanied Burgoyne. (National Archives of Canada – C-028244)

right spot, while an adverse wind could make the journey from Quebec to Montreal almost as long as that from Quebec to England.

The climate in eastern Canada was one of hot, humid summers and cold winters. Mean temperatures for both seasons fell nearer large stretches of water, such as the St Lawrence and the Great Lakes, but winter temperatures were invariably below freezing (exacerbated by the mini-ice age that gripped North America and Europe from 1650 to 1850). The area between Quebec and the Great Lakes also experienced the heaviest rainfall in Canada – and the autumn of 1775 would be no exception. Snowfall was often heavy, especially along the St Lawrence (even today aggregate falls of up to 20ft (6m) are common), but as this allowed the use of sleighs, it actually made land transportation easier.

PEOPLE

The British conquest of New France and the subsequent Treaty of Paris created a paradox – a "British" colony whose population was neither British, nor Protestant. Moreover, this population was used to absolute government that controlled every detail of their lives, and was now exposed to the 18th-century equivalent of liberal democracy.

By 1775, that population numbered between 200,000 and 250,000 souls. By far the largest (but rapidly decreasing) section was the "Indian" community that, including the remote Inuit, numbered around 150,000. The two main groups were the Six Nations (or Iroquois), traditional friends of the British living mainly around the Great Lakes, and the Seven Nations of the St Lawrence and Richelieu valleys. The latter had had the most contact with white society, and, consequently, had mainly converted to Christianity and become less warlike. However, their past allegiance to the French meant that they were still regarded with suspicion both by their white neighbors to the south and by the British authorities. The more bellicose group – the Iroquois – were increasingly divided in their loyalties. Other tribes in the Ohio–Mississippi corridor farther west still remembered Pontiac's War and distrusted all whites.

The white population numbered 75,000 in 1763, and natural growth and limited immigration had seen it expand to 90,000 by 1775. The relatively good quality of everyday life produced high birth and low death rates: typically 55–60 births and 30–40 deaths per 1,000 of population. Of the five main groups of whites, four were entirely French-speaking and Roman Catholic, and overwhelmingly Canadian born; the fifth was English-speaking, staunchly Protestant (or at least staunchly anti-Papist) and born outside Canada.

The largest of the four "French" groups was the *habitants* – mainly tenant farmers, with a few tradesmen (a lifestyle looked down on by all ranks of Quebec society). The second group was the *seigneury*, a transplanted aristocracy that had been augmented from time to time by civil and military officers arriving from France. In theory, they owned the land farmed by the *habitants*. The third group was the clergy, who were maintained by the tithes paid by the *habitants* and *seigneurs*. The fourth group was a tiny professional *elite* of notaries (lawyers), doctors, and merchants.

The fifth group, numbering 2,000, were of British origin, mainly from Scotland and the American colonies and usually referred to as "Old

NOVA SCOTIA

QUEBEC

Quebec
250

8,000

Trois Rivières
50

PROVINCE

Ottawa

Montréal
250

50
Chambly

St Johns

350
(dispersed)

St Lawrence

150

Great Lakes

Lake
Champlain

MASSACHUSETTS
(MAINE)

10
Crown Point
Fort Ticonderoga

50
Lake
George

Connecticut

NEW
HAMPSHIRE

8,000

Portsmouth

Mohawk

NEW YORK   20,000

Albany

Concord   Boston
4,000

MASSACHUSETTS

30,000

Hudson

Delaware

Ohio forts

200
(dispersed)

CONNECTICUT

20,000

New Haven

RHODE
ISLAND

Newport

6,000

N

PENNSYLVANIA

NEW
JERSEY

Long Island

New York City
100

ATLANTIC OCEAN

	British regulars
	Canadian militia (estimated strength)
	Colonial militia (estimated strength)
■	British garrison

0   50 miles
0   100 km

Canadian farmer, by F. von Germann c.1776. One British officer wrote: *"The dress of the natives is extremely well calculated for the climate; it consists ... of a blanket coat, a pair of what are called leggings, with a kind of flap on the outside of the leg, to prevent the snow from clogging around them; fur gloves, and a fur cap, which is made to pull over the ears ..."* The militia wore their own clothes, the only government-issue item being a stocking cap, or *tunque*, in blue (Montreal), white (Trois Rivières), or red (Quebec). The men received no pay, but were given arms and ammunition, and could buy their muskets at a discount on demobilization. In addition to military service, the men could also be called up for the *corvée* to perform public works, such as repairing roads, or transporting supplies. This caused great hardship and Carleton's decision to abolish it was welcomed. (New York Public Library)

Subjects" (in contrast to the French-speaking "New Subjects"). Apart from a few individuals settled near the frontier, almost all of them lived either in Quebec or Montreal.

POLITICS

Under French rule, the *habitants* had been part of the same feudal system found in metropolitan France, with the "noblesse" occupying all civil and military posts and the clergy holding sway over every public official up to and including the governor. However, by the 1750s the high cost of labor to manage the estates, the limited size and harsh realities of the Canadian economy, and the absence of the international political opportunities that existed in Europe, left many *seigneurs* poorer than their tenants, and even forced some to work their own land.

British rule had, entirely unintentionally, altered this dynamic still further, depriving the *seigneurs* and clergy of their political prominence and, with it, their last hold over the *habitants* (who became noticeably more spirited and independent – or rude and disobedient, depending on the observer's view). In fact, the *habitants* had become as independent-minded as the Americans – something that the *seigneurs* were quick to point out to their new rulers and that Americans saw as a weapon that they could use in their own struggle. For their part, the more educated and politicized *habitants* were eager to see who would triumph in the battle of wills between Great Britain and her other North American colonies.

Despite their numbers, the "Old Subjects" were extremely vociferous in demanding control of the political process in Canada, not least through their agents in London and the American colonies. About 400 of them were merchants, mainly in the fur trade, from which they had gradually displaced the French-speaking population, not without some bad feeling. They saw concessions to the majority as a threat to their right as British subjects to exploit any and every opportunity to make money – legal or otherwise. The first British governor, Major-General James Murray, saw most of them as "adventurers of mean education ... [with] ... their fortunes to make and little Sollicitous about the means," and his successor, Guy Carleton, held them in equal contempt.

Prominent among them was Thomas Walker, a Montreal merchant and former magistrate who seemed to thrive on persecution. In 1773 he encouraged the merchants of Quebec to form a committee, under John McCord, to draft a petition to Lord Dartmouth, Secretary of State for the Colonies, opposing the Quebec Bill. The petition attracted 61 signatures, not one of them from a French-speaking merchant. At the same time, Walker circulated a similar petition in Montreal that attracted 66 more. As it became increasingly obvious that the British government would frustrate their wishes, men such as McCord, Zachary Macaulay, John Dyer Mercier, Edward Antill and Udnay Hay in Quebec, Walker, James Price, William Heywood and Joseph Bindon in Montreal, and James Livingston and Moses Hazen at Chambly and St Johns, became an increasingly active fifth column. Many corresponded – often quite openly – with American politicians, and later with the commanders of the invading forces. Eventually, they would provide large sums of money and vital intelligence, or assist in recruiting other Canadians for the cause.

CHRONOLOGY

PRE-1773[2]

1534 Cartier claims the Gulf of St Lawrence for France
1608 Champlain founds Quebec City
1627 French merchants found the "Compagnie de la Nouvelle France"
1634 Trois Rivières founded
1642 Montreal founded
1663 Louis XIV establishes New France as a royal colony
1690 First British attack on Quebec repulsed by Frontenac
1711 British capture Quebec
1713 Treaty of Utrecht: British gain Acadia (Nova Scotia) and Newfoundland
1735 Completion of the "Chemin du Roi" linking Quebec and Montreal
1745 Army of New England provincial troops captures Louisburg
1754 French and Indian War begins
1758 Capture of Louisburg
1759 Wolfe captures Quebec
1760 Amherst captures Montreal
1763 Treaty of Paris; Pontiac's Rebellion; Proclamation Act
1768 Carleton succeeds Murray as Governor of Quebec
1773 American merchants organize to oppose Quebec Bill

1774

31 March Passing of the first of the Intolerable (Coercive) Acts
22 June Quebec Act receives Royal Assent
5 September First Continental Congress
18 September Carleton returns to Canada
4 December Sullivan raids Fort William and Mary
16 December Rhode Island militia seize Fort George

1775

19 April War begins at Lexington and Concord
8 May Green Mountain Boys rendezvous at Bennington
10 May Second Continental Congress
10 May Allen and Arnold capture Fort Ticonderoga
12 May Allen's men capture Crown Point
14 May Arnold leaves Skenesboro for St Johns
16 May Arnold captures St Johns
17 May Allen forced to abandon St Johns
25 June Schuyler appointed commander of Northern Department
27 June Congress authorizes invasion of Canada
18 July Schuyler arrives from New York City
24 July Schuyler sends Brown to Canada
28 August American forces leave Fort Ticonderoga
4 September Schuyler joins army at Ile-aux-Noix
5 September First attempt to capture St Johns
10 September Second attempt to capture St Johns
12 September Arnold's expedition leaves Cambridge
16 September Schuyler hands command over to Montgomery
18 September Third attempt to capture St Johns
19 September Arnold's force leaves Newburyport
27 September Allen captured outside Montreal
17 October Brown and Easton capture Chambly
27–30 October Carleton turned back at Longueuil
2 November St Johns surrenders
3 November Arnold reaches the St Lawrence
5 November Montgomery marches on Montreal
11 November Brown forces Prescott back to Montreal; Carleton escapes
13 November Montgomery enters Montreal; Arnold crosses the St Lawrence

15 November Arnold occupies the Plain of Abraham
19 November Carleton enters Quebec; Arnold retires to Pointe-aux-Trembles
2 December Montgomery arrives at Pointe-aux-Trembles
8 December Siege of Quebec begins
31 December Attack on Quebec; death of Montgomery

1776

1 January New England enlistments expire
8 March First reinforcements reach Arnold
1 April Wooster finally arrives at Quebec and assumes command
12 April Arnold leaves to take command at Montreal
19 April New York and Connecticut enlistments expire
29 April Franklin, Chase, and Carroll arrive at Montreal
1 May Thomas arrives at Quebec
2 May Thomas learns of British relief force
5 May Thomas orders withdrawal to Deschambaults
6 May *Isis* and *Surprise* arrive at Quebec
16 May Forster captures The Cedars
17 May Thomas arrives back at Sorel
20 May Forster ambushes Sherburn near The Cedars
26 May Negotiations between Forster and Arnold at Quinze Chiens
1 June Sullivan and Thompson arrive at Chambly with reinforcements
2 June Thomas dies of smallpox; Sullivan assumes command
8 June Action at Trois Rivières
9 June Arnold abandons Montreal
14 June Sullivan orders withdrawal to Ile-aux-Noix
17 June Arnold joins Sullivan at St Johns
24 June Sullivan orders abandonment of Ile-aux-Noix
4 July Declaration of Independence
5 July Schuyler and Gates arrive at Crown Point
7 July Survivors of Canadian expedition arrive at Crown Point
July–August Arnold's fleet constructed at Skenesboro
24 August Arnold's fleet leaves Crown Point
July–September Carleton's fleet constructed at St Johns
23 September Arnold's fleet in Valcour Sound
4 October Carleton's fleet leaves St Johns
11 October Carleton defeats Arnold at Valcour Island
12 October Arnold abandons three vessels at Schuyler's Island
13 October Remains of Arnold's fleet destroyed off Split Rock
14 October Americans burn and abandon Crown Point
16 October British troops land to attack Fort Ticonderoga
4 November Winter forces Carleton back to Canada

1777

June–October Burgoyne's expedition and Saratoga campaign
November Congressional committee considers second invasion

1778

January Preparations begun for second invasion
February Franco-American treaty of alliance signed
March Second invasion postponed indefinitely

---

2 Only events directly relevant to Canada are included here; for political and military events elsewhere in North America, see Campaign 37: *Boston 1775.*

THE OPPOSING COMMANDERS

Major-General Guy Carleton 1724–1808, Governor of Quebec. Tall, thin, and austere, Carleton typified the Irish Protestant upper class. His belief that Quebec could only be governed through tolerance earned him the enmity of Anglo-American merchants but also led him to overestimate the support that the *habitants* would give in the event of war. Despite his faults, Carleton's leadership kept Canada part of the British Empire and he is often seen as possibly the ablest British general of the war. (National Archives of Canada – C-002833)

THE BRITISH

Major-General Guy Carleton (1724–1808) entered the Army in May 1742 and by 1757 was a Captain-Lieutenant and Lieutenant-Colonel in the 1st Foot Guards. In 1758, he went to North America, serving at Louisburg and becoming quartermaster general to his friend, James Wolfe. With the local rank of colonel, he commanded the grenadiers at Quebec and was wounded. As an acting brigadier-general, he took part in the siege of Belle Ile in 1761, and later distinguished himself at Havana, where he was also wounded.

In 1766, he became Lieutenant Governor of Quebec and succeeded as Governor on Murray's recall to England in 1768, although his appointment was not officially confirmed until January 1775. From July 1770 to September 1774, Carleton was on leave in Great Britain, during which time he may have drafted the Quebec Bill. In 1772, he was promoted to major-general and became colonel of the 47th Foot.

When war came, Carleton had fewer than 1,000 Regulars to defend Canada, and this numerical inferiority and the growing realization that the *habitants* would not fight for the King, forced him to adopt a cautious strategy. Possibly he took this too far in refusing to allow any pursuit of the enemy following the failed attack on Quebec and demanding overwhelming superiority on Lake Champlain. However, on both occasions he was unsure of enemy numbers and knew that he would have to wait many months to replace any losses he incurred.

His long-running feud with Germain, aided by Burgoyne's scheming, and the failure to recapture Ticonderoga in 1776, led to his achievements being belittled in London. Nevertheless, his defense of Quebec earned him a knighthood (he was even allowed to wear the insignia and use the title before any official investiture) and he was made a lieutenant-general in August 1777. The appointment of Burgoyne to lead the invasion of New York led Carleton to resign in 1777, although he supported Burgoyne ably and remained in Canada until 1778.

In 1782, the Rockingham ministry chose Carleton to replace Clinton as the commander in chief in North America. He immediately removed corrupt military and civil officials, and stalled negotiations with Washington over the return of runaway slaves, allowing several thousand black Loyalists to flee to Canada. After supervising the evacuation of New York City in 1783, he was re-appointed Governor of Quebec in 1786, and made Baron Dorchester the same year. Apart from one two-year absence, he remained in Canada until 1796, returning home to live in retirement until his sudden death.

Brigadier-General Richard Prescott (1725–88) joined the Army in his teens and by 1756 was a major in the 33rd Foot. He served in Germany during the Seven Years War, becoming lieutenant-colonel of the 50th Foot in 1762. In 1773, he received the brevet rank of colonel, became acting colonel of the 7th Foot, and joined that regiment in Canada. At the outbreak of war, he was based at Montreal with the local rank of brigadier-general, making him Carleton's military deputy. Prescott supervised the reinforcement of St Johns and Chambly, but is better known for his mistreatment of Ethan Allen. During the evacuation of Montreal, he was bluffed into surrendering 11 vessels and over 120 troops, and spent almost a year in captivity, before being exchanged for John Sullivan in September 1776.

Two months later, he was confirmed as colonel of the 7th Foot and took part in the occupation of Newport, Rhode Island. In July 1777, he was captured again – this time in his own headquarters – as part of an American plan to release Charles Lee, for whom he was exchanged in May 1778. During this captivity, Prescott is supposed to have been horse-whipped by a tavern owner after insulting his wife's cooking. An unpleasant man, not even redeemed by military talent, Prescott provides a striking contrast to Carleton and MacLean. Yet despite being lampooned mercilessly by the British press, he became a major-general in 1777, and a lieutenant-general in 1782.

Lieutenant-Colonel Allan MacLean (1725–83) was born at Torloish in Scotland, and began his military service as a 17-year-old lieutenant in the Scots Brigade of the Dutch Army. Accounts differ as to which side he fought on in the Jacobite Rebellion of 1745, but he later transferred to the British Army, was commissioned in the 60th Foot (serving briefly as adjutant), and was badly wounded at the sieges of Ticonderoga and Fort Niagara. He served as a captain under Wolfe at the capture of Quebec (possibly in Montgomery's Highlanders), and later took command of a New York Independent Company. On the death of his wife in 1760, he returned to Scotland to care for his three daughters, and to raise the short-lived MacLean's Highlanders (114th Foot).

By 1775, MacLean was back in North America and was authorized by Gage to raise a regiment from Scottish communities in Canada, New York and the Carolinas. During Montgomery's invasion, he made two attempts to relieve St Johns, but was forced to return to Quebec, where he helped to stiffen the resolve of the civil population until Carleton's return from Montreal.

After 1776, MacLean held several administrative posts and in June 1777, he was made a brigadier-general and governor of Montreal. He also spent some time at Fort Niagara. MacLean served Carleton well in 1775 and had other subordinates been as industrious and aggressive, Montgomery may well have been stopped at St Johns.

Lieutenant-Colonel Allan MacLean 1725–83. MacLean, here wearing the uniform of the Royal Highland Emigrants, had raised a regiment for American service in the French and Indian War, (also generating debts that forced him to hide briefly among Jacobite exiles in France). He was largely responsible for stiffening the resolve of the inhabitants of Quebec and though he saw no action after 1776, is considered a hero in Canada today. He later became 22nd Chief of Clan MacLean and died in London. He was described by a colleague as "beloved, dreaded and indefatigable". (The Lord MacLean)

THE AMERICANS

Brigadier General Richard Montgomery (1738–75) was the third son of an Irish MP. Educated at Trinity College, Dublin, he became an ensign in the 17th Foot at 18 and in 1757 went to North America, serving at Louisburg,

Major-General John Burgoyne 1722–92, by Sir J. Reynolds. A cavalry officer and *bon vivant*, Burgoyne's reputation was based on a single action in Portugal in 1762. Given command of the troops sent to Canada in 1776, he helped Carleton to drive the Americans out of Canada, but agreed with Phillips and Fraser that more should have been done to recapture Ticonderoga before winter. Liked by the ordinary soldier for his humane views on discipline, he was not averse to undermining his superiors and played on Germain's dislike of Carleton to obtain command of the invasion of New York in 1777. (Frick Art Reference Library, New York City)

Major-General William Phillips RA 1731–81, by Francis Cotes. Phillips joined the artillery in 1746 and served with distinction in Germany, on Gibraltar, and as lieutenant governor of Windsor Castle. Sent to Canada to command the large artillery contingent of Burgoyne's army, his dynamism made him an indispensable second-in-command and the ideal man to supervise the construction of the Lake Champlain squadron. Captured at Saratoga in 1777, he was not exchanged until 1780, and died leading a raid into Virginia the following year. During his captivity, Thomas Jefferson described him as "the proudest man of the proudest nation on earth." (Frick Art Reference Library, New York City)

Ticonderoga, Crown Point, and Montreal. By 1760 he was adjutant of his regiment; he served at the capture of Martinique and Havanna in 1762, and ended the Seven Years War as a captain. After the Treaty of Paris, he remained in New York for two years, before returning to England in 1765, where he met prominent Whigs, such as Edmund Burke and Charles Fox.

By the early 1770s, Montgomery was disenchanted with the poor prospects of a peacetime army officer. In 1772, he sold his commission (having lost a chance to buy a majority in controversial circumstances) and emigrated to North America, buying a farm at King's Bridge, New York. In 1773, he married the daughter of prominent local landowner and judge Robert Livingston. This family connection opened doors and despite being resident in the Colonies for barely three years, Montgomery was appointed to represent Dutchess County at the New York Provincial Congress. In June 1775, the Provincial Congress nominated him for the post of brigadier general in the Continental Army. In both cases, his name was put forward without his knowledge and he only agreed to serve out of a sense of duty towards a community that had welcomed and befriended him.

Two months later, Montgomery found himself second-in-command of the Separate Army. Following Schuyler's withdrawal through illness, it was left to Montgomery to lead the inexperienced and undisciplined force into Canada. That leadership was enough to bring success at St Johns, but even he could not prevent his men leaving as their enlistments expired. His bravery eventually cost him his life at Quebec; when the British identified his corpse, it was buried with decency inside the walls of Quebec City.

Prior to his death, Montgomery had been promoted to the rank of major general, but was unaware of it when he led the assault on 31 December. He thus became the most senior Continental officer to be killed in action (Warren, killed at Bunker Hill, had been appointed a major general, but did not receive his commission). After Montgomery's death, he became the subject of Revolutionary verse and prose (including one work attributed to Thomas Paine), extolling his virtue and heroism – somewhat ironic given his reluctance to serve, either politically or militarily. His fate was also used to argue for extending periods of enlistment beyond one year. In 1787, a monument (made in Paris at the order of Benjamin Franklin) was erected in St Paul's church in New York City. In 1818, his body was exhumed, brought south and interred in the same church.

Brigadier General Benedict Arnold (1741–1801) was born in Norwich, Connecticut, the great-grandson of a governor of Rhode Island. As a young man, he courted physical danger and personality clashes, and was regarded by his peers as a natural leader. Apprenticed to a local apothecary, he soon set up his own business and later became a smuggler. As the political rift with Great Britain grew, these interests led him to oppose restrictions on trade, and he became a natural ally of the radicals.

By 1774, Arnold was a wealthy merchant, an accomplished sailor, and captain of the second company of the Connecticut Governor's Foot Guards. Within 24 hours of hearing of events at Lexington, he seized the New Haven powder magazine – upsetting a French and Indian War veteran named David Wooster in the process – and marched to Boston. Proposing the seizure of Fort Ticonderoga and its much-needed artillery and supplies, he was given a commission by Massachusetts, which was later rescinded, much to his annoyance. In June, the death of his wife forced him to return to New Haven, where he was laid low by an attack of gout. He then received a third blow when the Massachusetts Congress refused to pay most of the expenses he claimed to have incurred in its service.

In September, General George Washington persuaded him to command one of the expeditions into Canada. The march to Quebec and the attack on the city illustrated his dynamic leadership, but the legal problems that followed his period as governor of Montreal showed another side to his character (as would a similar post in Philadelphia after the Saratoga campaign). He became embroiled in a court-martial instigated by Brown, Easton, and Hazen following the mysterious loss of supplies Arnold had seized from local merchants and sent to St Johns. When the court refused to hear one of his witnesses, Arnold challenged the members to a duel and only the intervention of Gates prevented further unpleasantness.

Arnold was a complex character: the creation of the Lake Champlain fleet showed his immense dynamism, the attack on Quebec his bravery (both traits that would surface again at Saratoga). However, avarice and "creative" accounting skills led to controversy throughout his Continental service, and also after the war, while his sensitivity to personal slights – real or imagined – contributed as much to his decision to change sides as his flirtations with the Loyalists in Philadelphia.

Major General John Sullivan (1740–95) was born in Somersworth, New Hampshire, the son of Irish immigrants. He practiced law and was reputedly so greedy and litigious that he was once attacked by a mob. Despite this, he became a major in the militia and was elected to both the First and Second Continental Congress, aligning himself with the radicals and welcoming a split with Great Britain.

In December 1774 he seized 100 barrels of powder from Fort William and Mary in Portsmouth, promised the Governor that his followers would disperse, and then promptly went back and took 60 muskets and 15 cannon. Seven months later, he was sent to Boston with the rank of

Brigadier-General Simon Fraser 1729–77, by James Watson. As lieutenant-colonel of the 24th Foot, he brought the regiment to a high standard of efficiency, resulting in his appointment to lead the Advance Corps – the *élite* of Burgoyne's army. His performance at Trois Rivières and in the subsequent pursuit of Sullivan, suggest a high level of competence – a view confirmed the following year up to his death at Saratoga. (National Archives of Canada – C-008649)

Major General Richard Montgomery, 1738–75, by C.W. Peale. Despite being a New Yorker, he never suffered the mistrust and insubordination that Schuyler endured from the New Englanders. He appears to have been a reluctant rebel and his death may well have been timely for all concerned with the cause of independence. (Independence National Historical Park)

brigadier general, but also remained active in politics, campaigning for a distinct government for New Hampshire. After the British evacuation, he was ordered to Canada with six regiments, but soon found himself in command of an army facing the twin scourges of smallpox and a superior enemy. Attempting to take the offensive, faulty intelligence led to the defeat at Trois Rivières, after which he saw retreat as the only option. He withdrew to Crown Point, only to find that he had been replaced by Gates.

After complaining to Congress in person, Sullivan returned to take command on Long Island, only to be superseded again – this time by Putnam – and then captured at Brooklyn. He was exchanged in September for Richard Prescott, served under Washington in the New Jersey and Pennsylvania campaigns, and commanded at Rhode Island (1778) and against the Iroquois (1779). Illness contracted during the latter campaign forced him to resign his commission and enter Congress. He chaired the inquiry into the 1781 mutinies, and later became governor of New Hampshire and a federal judge.

THE OPPOSING FORCES

THE BRITISH AND THEIR ALLIES

The "British" forces comprised six distinct elements. In order of size, they were the Army ("Regulars"), the German Auxiliaries, the Militia (predominantly French-speaking Canadians), the Royal Navy, Indians, and Loyalists (i.e. loyal white civilians of British, Irish or American birth).

The Army[3]

In 1775, this element of imperial defense was in short supply everywhere in North America. Of the five infantry regiments assigned to Canada, two – the 10th and 52nd Foot – had gone to Boston in October 1774 on the assumption that 3,000 militia would mobilize to oppose any invasion. This left the 8th Foot dispersed around the Great Lakes posts, and the 7th and 26th Foot – both at least ten percent under strength – defending the Province of Quebec. The 26th and all but two companies of the 7th were captured in November 1775, and spent over a year in captivity.

In May 1776, the 29th Foot arrived at Quebec, and in June, eight more regiments arrived from Europe (the 9th, 20th, 21st, 24th, 31st, 34th, 53rd, and 62nd Foot) and one (the 47th Foot) from Halifax. Of these ten units only the 47th Foot had seen action since 1762 (at Concord and Bunker Hill), although the 29th, 31st, and 34th Foot had all served in North America during the early 1770s. However, the light companies of the five senior regiments had trained in the new tactics devised by Sir William Howe in 1774, and were prominent in the 1776 campaign.

Burgoyne also brought four companies of artillery. Prior to that, Carleton had only a single company of regular gunners, most of whom were captured at St Johns.

German Auxiliaries

Most of the German contingent in Canada came from Brunswick (Braunschweig-Wolfenbüttel), with one infantry regiment and an artillery company from Hesse-Hanau. The first division of 2,282 Brunswickers and 668 Hessians arrived in June; the second division, 2,000 Brunswickers, arrived in September. During 1776, only the artillerymen saw serious action, primarily at Valcour Island, where they manned two gunboats and some ordnance on *Thunderer*, and performed creditably. Von Riedesel used the winter of 1776 to adapt the tactics and clothing of the entire corps to North American conditions.

The Militia

Following the acquisition of New France in the Treaty of Paris in 1763, the British by and large retained the administrative infrastructure, including the militia. Each parish provided a company of men when required by the

Major General John Sullivan 1740–95, by R.M. Staigg. Though brave and a sound organizer, Sullivan could be guilty of overconfidence and was easily dismayed by adversity. He also courted popularity among officers and men alike, and was easily impressed by flattery, as the Howes demonstrated when they talked him into taking a peace proposal to Congress. His rank and the length of his military career are surprising given his distinct lack of success (apart from the Iroquois raids of 1779) and probably owed much to his political astuteness. He survived a court of inquiry after Brandywine, avoided one completely over the Newport fiasco, threatened to resign over the promotion of De Coudray, and may have been involved in the Conway Cabal (if it existed). (Independence National Historical Park)

Major General Horatio Gates 1728–1806, by C.W. Peale. Gates entered the British Army in 1744 and saw action in the French and Indian War, before retiring to Virginia as a half-pay major. There he met George Washington, who recommended him to the post of adjutant general of the Continental Army in June 1775. (Independence National Historical Park)

Philip Schuyler 1733–1804, after J. Trumbull. Schuyler was a veteran of the French and Indian War, which taught him the importance of logistics to any force operating in the northern wilderness. In 1775, he was appointed major general and commander of the Northern Department, but his methodical approach and views on military discipline alienated the New England contingent. (Independence National Historical Park)

authorities, based on a fixed quota (leaving enough men to maintain farming and business). From 1759, there were three administrative "brigades" based on Montreal, Trois Rivières, and Quebec. All males between 16 and 60 years old were eligible. On paper, 15,000 men were available to France in the previous conflict, but only a third were mobilized at any time, of whom 80 percent were employed in transport and supply. In 1775, Carleton's lack of Regulars led the militia to form the bulk of every combat formation in the field. Never enthusiastic, the militia was further de-motivated by Carleton's apparent lack of aggression, and if not employed immediately tended to go home.

The Quebec City militia – effectively a separate force – was mobilized in September 1775, and served until May 1776 (but continued to attend parades and social events until 1783). There were 11 companies of "Canadian Militia" (reduced to eight in December), six companies of English-speaking colonists, or "British Militia", and one company of artillery.

The Royal Navy

The senior service was involved in most actions of the campaign. A detachment from the schooner *Gaspé* served at St Johns, albeit less than impressively. At Quebec, nine companies were formed from the crews of the warships and merchantmen in the harbor, whilst the frigate *Lizard* and the "snow" *Fell* were moored in the St Lawrence to command the river.

In 1776, 700 men were drafted from the fleet that relieved Quebec, to man the Lake Champlain flotilla. Whilst Arnold's fleet usually attracts all the attention, the breakdown, transportation, and reassembly of the four major British vessels was a far more impressive technical achievement.

Indians

Lord Dartmouth sanctioned the use of Indians in July 1775 – a move that generated much controversy at the time, and more as the war progressed (although Congress had authorized the raising of a "minuteman" company from Stockbridge warriors four months earlier). Military and civil control was exercised via the Department of Indian Affairs, established in 1754 to counter French superiority in this aspect of colonial warfare. There were two districts – north and south – each with a superintendent reporting to the commander in chief in North America.

In 1775, the northern district, under Guy Johnson, ran from Canada to the Pennsylvania–Virginia border. It contained around 8,500 warriors, but few of these were available initially, as the invasion isolated the western and southern tribes until late 1776. The main sources of manpower available to Carleton were the Iroquois (or Six Nations) of the Mohawk Valley, and Caughnawaga (Seven Nations) of the St Lawrence Valley. The Iroquois were traditional allies of the British, but the Caughnawaga had previously served the French and were believed (with some justification) to be lukewarm. In fact, both groups were the focus of efforts by Congress – including visits by their Stockbridge "brothers" – to negotiate their neutrality. A few Oneida and Tuscarora actually fought against the British).

Carleton was the only senior British officer in North America to speak out against using them, as much for military as humanitarian reasons. Their fearsome reputation was a double-edged sword and their unique approach to warfare – based on returning home with as much loot and as few casualties as possible – made controlling them a problem. Nevertheless, they were invaluable as scouts: Carleton employed 50 warriors in this role in mid-1775, and over 640 led his advance into New York a year later. War parties usually operated under the direction of officers of the Indian Department (often seconded Regulars), French militia officers or local Army officers. Tactically, they were by no means naive: the Iroquois employed a rudimentary form of "fire and movement" and were adept at using cover to close with the enemy. Whilst acts of cruelty were committed occasionally, most of the atrocities ascribed to them – for example, at The Cedars – were either exaggerated, or completely false, often being used to justify attacks and land-grabbing by colonists.

Loyalists

Dozens of English-speaking Canadians served as volunteers, but the only formal unit of white Loyalists was the Royal Highland Emigrants (later the 84th Foot). Originally two separate corps, it soon became a two-battalion regiment, recruiting in every colony, and even direct from Scotland (being a Provincial unit, this was illegal, but MacLean circumvented the law by having native Scots swear the oath after arriving in America). Numbers were high thanks to unusually generous bounties, the use of traditional Highland dress, and the patronage of their first colonel, Gage, who prevented "poaching" by other units.

The regiment fought in every major action of the campaign, except Valcour Island, usually with distinction, particularly at St Johns and Quebec. It remained on the Provincial establishment until 24 December 1778, and on 10 April 1779, company strength was officially increased from 50 rank-and-file to 70. By 1783, the unit had served everywhere from the Great Lakes to Nova Scotia and from the North Atlantic to Florida. The only blot on its record was the high desertion rate of men recruited from the Continentals captured at Quebec which, along with Burgoyne's dislike of MacLean, saw the unit left in Canada during the 1777 campaign.

THE AMERICANS

In contrast to their enemy, the American forces in Canada changed composition, personnel, and organization frequently. The expiry of enlistments led to the consolidation of the remaining men into ad hoc "regiments" (often no bigger than companies), and unit numbers and titles were recycled.

On 14 June 1775, Congress adopted an "American continental army" of 10,000 (later 22,000) men at Boston, and 5,000 more at New York City. The latter came mainly from New York and Connecticut. In theory, all of the units in Canada were adopted by Congress, and so qualify as "Continentals" – the equivalent of British Regulars. However, even as late as 1776, a standing army was still anathema to many politicians and units were considered to be on loan to Congress. Thus, political control remained with "the people" through the colonial legislatures. The force that entered Canada was known as the "Separate Army" until the end of 1775, and thereafter as the "Northern Army". Commanded by Schuyler, it had its own quartermaster general, paymaster general, military secretary,

Brigadier General David Wooster 1711–77. Had served in the French and Indian War, and in 1775 was commander of the Connecticut contingent of the Continental Army. He served reluctantly under Schuyler and was Montgomery's second-in-command at St Johns. Left in charge of Montreal, he soon displayed the worst aspects of his character. He was killed during the British raid on Danbury in 1777. (Anne S K Brown Military Collection)

RIGHT **Private of the Royal Highland Emigrants, by F. von Germann c.1776. This corps was to have the same uniforms and accoutrements as the 42nd (Royal Highland) Regiment. However, most men wore civilian clothes until November 1775 at least. They were to ... *engage during the present troubles in America only. Each soldier to have two hundred acres of land in any province in North America, he shall think proper, the King to pay the Patent fees, Secretary's fees and Surveyors General, besides twenty years free of quit rent, each married man gets fifty acres for his wife, and fifty for each child, of the same terms. And as a gratuity besides the above great terms, one guinea levy money...* (New York Public Library)**

This soldier in winter clothing, by . von Germann c.1776, shows typical winter dress for British Regulars (and also Continentals during the winter of 1775, after Montgomery purchased large amounts of winter clothing at Montreal). (New York Public Library)

engineers (three), and hospital services, the last run by Schuyler's personal physician, Dr Samuel Stringer.

Initially, each colony had its own regimental structure, usually based on the ten-company British battalion (but without flank companies). However, on the reorganization of the Continental Army in early 1776, ten colonies adopted a common battalion structure, often called the "November" model. This had a colonel, lieutenant colonel, and major, plus ten regimental staff, with just eight companies, each of four officers, four sergeants, four corporals, two musicians, and 76 privates. The other three colonies – New Jersey, Delaware, and Pennsylvania – adopted the "October" model, which had the same regimental headquarters, but only three officers (captain, lieutenant, and ensign), four sergeants, and 68 privates per company.

At the same time, the rifle unit raised by Congress in June 1775 and all the New England infantry were amalgamated into a single "Continental Line" of 26 consecutively numbered regiments. An artillery regiment was also formed, under Henry Knox, with 12 companies, each comprising a captain, a captain-lieutenant, a first lieutenant, two second lieutenants, four sergeants, four corporals, eight bombardiers, eight gunners, 32 matrosses (privates), and a drummer and fifer. Two companies (under Ebenezer Stevens and Benjamin Eustis) went to Canada in early 1776.

New Hampshire [4]

Because of its frontier status, New Hampshire contained many French and Indian War veterans, particularly from "ranging" (scouting) units. With its "line" regiments at Boston, the colony's main contribution to the Separate Army was a ranger detachment under Captain (later Major) Timothy Bedel. Originally a single company of state troops, it expanded to three companies, each of 66 officers and men, and served until December 31.

After the defeat at Quebec, Congress sent urgent requests to New Hampshire, Massachusetts, and Connecticut for extra regiments, over and above their agreed quotas, to serve for one year in Canada (in each case the units were recruited from the counties closest to Canada). On 20 January 1776, the ranger unit was re-raised in north-west New Hampshire, again under Bedel (now a colonel), but this time with eight companies. After the British evacuated Boston in March 1775, the 2nd, 5th, and 8th Continental Regiments (formerly the 3rd, 1st, and 2nd New Hampshire regiments of 1775) were sent to Canada. Averaging over 500 men, only the battalions from Pennsylvania were larger.

Massachusetts

Although Massachusetts' forces were fully committed to the siege of Boston until March 1776, it did raise one provisional regiment, under Colonel Elisha Porter, to serve in Canada. Organized as a standard Continental battalion, it may have reached 500 effectives. Once the British evacuated Boston, the 15th, 24th, and 25th Continental regiments were also sent north.

Connecticut

After Allen and Arnold had gone, only a few local militia were left to guard Ticonderoga, so Congress assumed responsibility for some of

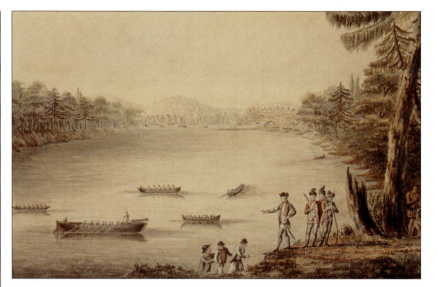

British boats on Lake Champlain, by William Hunter c.1777. Although they depict events from Burgoyne's expedition the following year, these two views of British troops and vessels are equally appropriate to the 1776 campaign. Behind men of Fraser's Advance Corps are various bateaux, and a longboat armed with a 2-pdr. (National Archives of Canada – C-001524)

British troops on Lake Champlain, by William Hunter c.1777. Various bateaux and other vessels, with a gunboat second from right. These were about 35ft (10.6m) long, 12ft (3.6m) in the beam, and carried one cannon in the bow, ranging from a 6-pdr to 24-pdr. Though equipped with a sail, rowing was the more common form of propulsion. (National Archives of Canada – C-001525)

RIGHT American private, by F. von Germann c.1776. Few units in the Northern Army had uniforms and of those that did, few had more than one or two companies dressed alike. The inherent "independence" of the enlisted man produced a stubborn indiscipline and laxity that, in action, could result in either blind panic, or stubborn heroism. One-year enlistments prevented the establishment of an experienced *cadre*, or the development of *esprit de corps* within any unit, whilst disease (especially smallpox) and a constant lack of essential supplies, destroyed the soldier's will to fight as certainly as it did his constitution. (New York Public Library)

Connecticut's forces and sent them to defend it. This contingent comprised three of Connecticut's six (later eight) regiments – the 1st, 4th, and 5th. All ranks were drawn from existing militia companies, in proportion to the population of each county, and had to serve until 10 December. As with all the New England contingents raised in 1775, these regiments were outside the militia system and were more akin to the Provincial units of earlier colonial wars.

Infantry regiments had six staff officers, plus a colonel, lieutenant colonel, and major (the 1st had two majors as its colonel, David Wooster, was also a general) and ten companies, each with four sergeants, four corporals, two musicians, and 90 privates. Seven companies had four officers, the other three being nominally commanded by the three "field" officers (hence Wooster had to fulfill three roles). Two companies each of the 1st and 4th regiments remained at Boston.

In early January 1776, Colonel Samuel Elmore formed a provisional regiment at Quebec from men whose enlistments had not expired, or who had re-enlisted. In response to urgent requests from Congress, another

regiment was raised in January 1776, by Colonel Charles Burrall; this included one company trained as artillerymen, under Captain John Bigelow.

New York

In 1775, New York raised four infantry regiments and an artillery company, with a total strength of 3,000 men. The gunners, under Captain John Lamb, came almost entirely from New York City, and were clothed in blue faced buff to avoid being mistaken for lowly infantrymen. After 31 December, almost all of the survivors re-enlisted in a new company under Lieutenant Isaiah Wool. In 1776, two new companies were formed in New York City, and assigned to Schuyler.

The infantry regiments were recruited from New York City, Albany and the Mohawk Valley, the northern Hudson valley, and the southern Hudson Valley, respectively. The 1st included several officers who had fought in the French and Indian War, while the 2nd had a strong Dutch influence.

Each regiment had 758 men, comprising a colonel, lieutenant colonel, and major, five "staff" (adjutant, quartermaster, surgeon, surgeon's mate, and chaplain), and ten companies, each with a captain, three lieutenants, three sergeants, three corporals, a drummer, a fifer, and 64 privates. Companies were based on existing militia units, whose own precedence determined each regiment's seniority, and the regiments tended to represent the majority politics – radical, or conservative – of these areas.

In April 1776, another four (later five) infantry regiments were raised, also numbered 1st to 4th. Three incorporated veterans of the 1775 campaign, but apparently only the 1st corresponded to its 1775 counterpart, the 2nd being based on the old 3rd and the 3rd around the old 4th. The 4th was a new unit, raised in Albany, whilst the old 2nd eventually became the 5th Regiment. Colonel John Nicholson also formed a provisional battalion at Quebec from the men remaining after the expiry of the second tranche of enlistments in April 1776, but the unit was disbanded and the men transferred to another regiment based in the Mohawk Valley (both of these corps employing three-year enlistments).

New Jersey

New Jersey raised three infantry regiments during the winter of 1775. Initially intended for Washington's Main Army, they were diverted to reinforce Schuyler, the 2nd arriving in Canada in March, and the 1st in May (the 3rd went to the Mohawk Valley). The two senior regiments were based on existing militia structures, the 1st recruiting in the north-east and the 2nd in the south-west; the 3rd appears to have been recruited "at large". Both the New Jersey and Pennsylvania contingents included a number of French and Indian War veterans.

Pennsylvania

Pennsylvania, not being a Royal colony, had no established militia, but formed volunteer units – "Associators" – during the 1770s. In January 1776, six infantry units (referred to as battalions, rather than regiments) were authorized, of which the 1st, 2nd, 4th, and 6th served in Canada. One of their conditions of service was that they operated as a single brigade, under a Pennsylvanian general. One of the eight companies in each battalion consisted of riflemen, which brought complaints from officers concerned at how an asymmetrical seven-company unit would maneuver when the riflemen were detached. A seventh battalion – named after its commander, Colonel Aenas Mackay – was raised in the summer of 1776 to help defend the frontier of the Northern Department.

Due to a misunderstanding, Pennsylvania also formed an artillery company, which Congress later agreed to adopt. The unit was recruited by the engineer, Bernard Romans and led into Canada by Captain-Lieutenant Gibbs Scott.

Canada

While Congress gradually adopted the regular units raised by each colony, various "special" units were also recruited for Canada. Some, such as Duggan's Corps, were never completed and a few only ever existed on paper. Among the more organized were the Green Mountain Boys from the New Hampshire Grants (now Vermont). Raised illegally before the war to defend the Grants from incursions by New Yorkers, its knowledge of wilderness fighting prompted Congress to let Schuyler formalize the unit as a seven-company battalion, each with three officers and 70 men, commanded by a lieutenant colonel and a major.

American riflemen. Contemporary depiction of enemy troops by a German officer. Though feared by the British at first, the rifle was soon found to have limitations, even in the hands of frontiersmen. A slow rate of fire and the inability to take a bayonet left the rifleman vulnerable to well-trained, musket-armed opponents. (Private collection)

At the end of 1775, Congress formally authorized the creation of an eight-company unit from the Canadians recruited by Livingston during the autumn. This later became the 1st Canadian Regiment, and included former soldiers of the *Compagnies Franche de la Marine* who had settled in Canada. Being French born, rather than Canadian, they were less reluctant to fight the British. The 1st Canadian Regiment appears to have peaked at 200 all ranks.

The 2nd Canadian Regiment was authorized in February 1776 and raised at Montreal by Moses Hazen. It adopted a French regimental structure, having a colonel and lieutenant colonel, and four battalions, each commanded by a major, and containing five companies of three officers and 50 enlisted men. However, probably only one battalion was ever raised. Because Hazen was never reimbursed for the costs of recruiting the unit, he retained proprietary control, hence the unit survived the disbandment of the more senior 1st Canadian Regiment, retained its French structure, and later had the pick of the foreigners in the Continental Army.

Arnold's command

The 1,100 men who marched through Maine were all volunteers (in fact, so many volunteered that they had to be chosen by lot). There were two, five-company battalions of musketeers, drawn from all four New England colonies, and three companies of riflemen – two of Pennsylvanians, one of Virginians – drawn from the rifle regiment raised by Congress. These latter were frontiersmen, ideally equipped for the journey: some Pennsylvanians marched 450 miles (725km) in 26 days to reach Boston; the Virginians covered 600 (965km) miles in three weeks.

The two New England battalions were led by lieutenant colonels Christopher Greene (brother of Nathaniel) and Roger Enos. Greene was 38, a former militia major, who owned sawmills and forges in Rhode Island; Enos, 46, was a veteran of the French and Indian War. Their deputies were majors Timothy Bigelow, a Massachusetts blacksmith, and Return Jonathan Meigs, of Connecticut. The ten captains included Henry Dearborn, a young doctor and veteran of Bunker Hill; Simeon Thayer, a wig maker and former Roger's Ranger; Samuel Ward, the son of a former governor of Rhode Island and just 19, and William Goodrich, who had connections with the Stockbridge tribe. The riflemen were led by Daniel Morgan, and two wildly contrasting Pennsylvanians – Matthew Smith, a hard drinker and fighter, and the quiet, courteous William Hendricks.

Arnold also had a small staff – his secretary, Eleazer Oswald; the brigade major, Danish engineer Christian Febiger; a chaplain, the 29-year-old firebrand Samuel Spring; Dr Isaac Senter, seven years younger and one of the first surgeons appointed to the Continental Army; and Aaron Burr, described by John Hancock as a "gentleman of reputation." Two women also accompanied the expedition; both were wives of Pennsylvanian riflemen and, apparently, every bit as tough.

Arnold's fleet on Lake Champlain consisted of 17 vessels – three schooners, one sloop, one cutter, two row galleys, two galleys, and eight "gundalows" (gondolas). Of these, 15 fought at Valcour; of the other two, one schooner was converted to carry stores and act as a hospital ship, and one "gundalow" was still fitting out at Skenesboro. Due to the difficulties in recruiting experienced sailors willing to take on the Royal Navy, most of the crews were soldiers, including a draft of 300 men from two New Hampshire regiments. It is unclear how near Arnold got to his official complement of 915 men, although the "gundalow" *Philadelphia* apparently was missing only one man from its establishment of 45.

---

3 Detailed information on the organization of British infantry regiments can be found in Campaign 37: *Boston 1775* and on the Brunswick and Hesse-Hanau troops in Campaign 67: *Saratoga 1777*.
4 These contingents are listed by colony, in the order of precedence later adopted by the Continental Army, ie geographically north to south, with Canada last.

ENTER THE LIBERATORS

THE DECISION TO INVADE

For three weeks, Congress discussed handing back Ticonderoga and Crown Point, and disavowing Allen and Arnold. Another letter was sent to Canada, referring to despotism, tyranny, oppression, and common cause, and on 1 June, Congress declared that an invasion of Canada was contrary to its aims. However, by mid-June the delegates had been persuaded that invasion was a strategic necessity. Both Allen and Arnold had suggested that it would require just 2,000 men and, if reports of British weakness and the strength of pro-American feeling were true, the capture of Montreal and Quebec were assured.

Arnold's plan involved a siege of St Johns by 700 troops, with another 1,000 bypassing the fort to seize Montreal (with the gates opened by sympathizers), and 300 more guarding the lines of communication along Lake Champlain and the Richelieu. With Montreal captured, St Johns, Chambly, and Quebec could not hold out and Congress would control the entire Province long before reinforcements could arrive, removing any threat of a British counterattack. The plan appealed to both Congress and to General Washington, and the invasion was approved on 27 June, but with the New Yorkers Schuyler and Montgomery, rather than the Yankee Arnold, in command.

South view of Ile-aux-Noix, by Henry Rudyerd c.1780. Deriving its name from the plentiful nut trees, the island was a mile and a half (2.4km) in length, and three-quarters of a mile (1.3km) wide. This view was painted by an engineer officer late in 1776, after the Americans retreat and the construction of a series of blockhouses each able to hold 100 men and four guns (two on each floor). (National Archives of Canada – C-040355)

When Schuyler reached Ticonderoga on 18 July, he was confronted by utter chaos. Not only did the few troops present lack even the rudiments of discipline (and, moreover, have no intention of learning them from a haughty New Yorker), but the logistical systems so dear to his heart – and essential to wilderness warfare – were nonexistent. His experiences as deputy quartermaster general in the French and Indian War helped to remedy some defects, but it was the end of August before a very "rough and ready" Separate Army left Ticonderoga, and 2 September before it set foot on Canadian soil.

When Carleton learned of the loss of Ticonderoga and Crown Point, he placed his lieutenant governor, Hector Cramahé, in charge at Quebec and left for Montreal with Major Joseph Stopford and most of the 7th Foot. At Montreal he found under 600 Regulars fit for duty, an indifferent and insubordinate militia, no armed vessels, no fort in good enough repair to withstand a siege, no immediate prospect of reinforcements, and a small but influential body of citizens openly consorting with the enemy. The *seigneury* soon rallied round, and the younger English colonists volunteered to serve at St Johns, but the *habitants* appeared "badly disposed." A proclamation by Bishop Briand of Quebec, urging them to ignore American propaganda and serve the King, elicited little response beyond the denunciation of the Bishop as a traitor. On 9 June, acting on advice from a leading *seigneur*, Carleton established martial law and called out the militia (though he was not optimistic about the response). Unfortunately, he made the mistake of choosing new senior officers from the nobility who had military experience but only in the regular French army. With no knowledge of the militia, they granted commissions to friends and relatives and ignored the existing officers. Not surprisingly, many were physically abused and chased out of the parishes.

The English-speaking colonists were no more helpful: barely 70 men appeared when the "British Militia" of Quebec were called out. Carleton could understand the reluctance of the "New Subjects", but the behaviour of the "Old Subjects" left him incensed. Frustrated, he turned to a community he knew he could rely upon: the former Highland soldiers settled in Nova Scotia and the Mohawk Valley, who were being recruited by

MacLean. Somewhat less welcome was the "reinforcement" from Boston – Brigadier-General Richard Prescott. Carleton gave him command of the Montreal garrison, but otherwise tried to ignore him.

As if all of this was not enough, Carleton also had problems with the Indians, alarmed at American success and nervous of an invasion. Gage and others were insistent that they be used and so Carleton wrote to the posts at Detroit, Kaskaskia, and Michillimackinac, warning them of rebel activity and suggesting that they took steps to ensure the loyalty of local tribes. Guy Johnson, superintendent of the northern Indian Department, met Carleton at Lachine on 26 July, along with over 1,600 warriors who expressed a desire to lay waste New England. They were appalled when Carleton declined the offer and forbade them to cross the frontier, and Johnson, along with Joseph Brant and an Indian Department officer, Daniel Claus, went to England to seek permission for a more aggressive posture. An attempt by Carleton to placate the tribes by taking 50 warriors as scouts made no impact. Some, mainly Onondaga and St Regis, drifted home but others craved action. On 22 August, a group under the Chevalier François de Lorimier attacked some of Allen's men near the Lacolle River. Several Indians were wounded and one of Allen's officers – Remember Baker – was killed, at which Congress immediately sent a Stockbridge delegation to the Caughnawaga to explain that the clash had been accidental and that the Americans intended them no harm.

Meanwhile, Carleton had turned his attention to the forts. He could not afford to yield territory, especially as Montreal only had a weak wall and ditch, therefore the defense had to be based near the frontier, so he ordered repairs to the defenses at St Johns and garrisoned it with as many Regulars and volunteers as he could find. He also sent to Halifax for carpenters and shipwrights and to Gage in Boston for the return of the 10th and 52nd Foot, so that he could chase the enemy back down Lake Champlain once they were defeated. However, when *Liberty* and *Enterprise* returned to St Johns and bombarded it on 7 June, Carleton knew that he faced an invasion by a buoyant enemy and that he had insufficient resources to repel it. Everything rested on St Johns: if it fell

East view of the north and south redoubts at St Johns ... from the block-house erected on the opposite side of the river 1776, by Henry Rudyerd. The original French works comprised two earth redoubts surrounding a barrack block and a stone house respectively. An engineer officer Captain John Marr, rebuilt the works in the summer of 1775, linking the redoubts with a palisaded communication trench, and fronting them with a seven-foot ditch on all but the river-facing side. This view and the previous one show the post after its reconstruction, following the defeat of Sullivan's army in June 1776, but it would not have looked much different in September 1775. (National Archives of Canada – C-001503)

he would lose most of his Regulars and Montreal, leaving just Quebec standing between the Americans and control of Canada.

ST JOHNS AND CHAMBLY

Captain John Lamb 1735–1800, artist unidentified. An optical instrument maker and wine merchant, Lamb became heavily involved in radical politics in New York City, and on the outbreak of war took command of an independent artillery company. Sent to the Northern Department, he incurred the displeasure of Schuyler by continuing his political activities after the war, he was an ardent anti-Federalist). He was badly wounded during the attack on Quebec and quickly paroled, but not formally exchanged in January 1777. Later appointed colonel of the 2nd Continental Artillery, he ended the war as a brevet brigadier general, and was later appointed a customs collector by Washington. (Anne S.K. Brown Military Collection)

The plan approved by Congress involved a two-pronged attack to make Carleton disperse his forces. The left wing, 3,000 men under Schuyler, would head for Montreal, via Lake Champlain and the Richelieu River. The right wing, 1,050 men led by Arnold, would head up the Kennebec River, over Height of Land, and down the Chaudiere River to Quebec. This "second front" was not Arnold's idea, but he quickly became a supporter once denied command of the main force.

Montgomery set out from Crown Point with 1,500 men on 30 August and by 2 September was at Ile-aux-Noix, where Schuyler joined him two days later. Despite poor health, Schuyler was determined to lead his men into Canada, which he did on 5 September. As his boats approached St Johns, British guns opened fire but did little damage, and the troops landed in a swamp about a mile from the fort. As they advanced on the fort they were ambushed by 100 Indians under Lorimier. Overcoming the initial shock, Schuyler's men fought back, with Lorimier losing four dead and five wounded. Disgruntled at the lack of support from the garrison, the Indians withdrew. By evening the Americans had built a breastwork beside the river, but later had to pull back as the British gunners found the range.

That night, Moses Hazen (posing as a friend of Congress) informed Schuyler that the fort had plenty of troops and supplies, a heavily armed schooner – *Royal Savage* – was heading his way, and there was little support for the invasion among the *habitants*. The last point was of particular concern, as Schuyler had believed it was the one element he could count on. After a council of war, Schuyler pulled back to Ile-aux-Noix the next day. Scarcely had he arrived and informed Congress indicating that he was considering withdrawing to Crown Point, when James Livingston – an American living near Chambly and a distant relative of Montgomery's wife – arrived and presented an entirely different picture. Urging one more effort against St Johns, Livingston promised that the Canadians would join Schuyler.

Schuyler now had 1,900 men, but only 1,000 fit for action. They re-embarked and headed back to St Johns, this time under Montgomery. Early on 10 September they reoccupied the works built during the previous attack and a group from the 1st New York entered the woods west of the fort, with the aim of cutting the supply line to Chambly. The earlier experience with the Indians had made the men jumpy, and a chance encounter in the dark woods led two groups to fire on each other. Eventually, the problem was sorted out, but then Ritzema's men faced a real ambush and fled to the river. As Montgomery rallied them in person, a rumor began that *Royal Savage* was about to bombard them and he was forced to shepherd them back onto the bateaux and return to Ile-aux-Noix.

A third attempt was scheduled for 13 September, but the weather intervened. Schuyler again fell ill and, on 16 September, handed over command to Montgomery. Determined to make the most of this **33**

THE SIEGE OF ST JOHNS, SEPTEMBER–NOVEMBER 1775
(pages 34–35)

Following two unsuccessful attempts to capture the British post at St Johns, the Rebel army returned on 16 September and began a formal siege. Initially, progress was slow as the besiegers lacked heavy artillery and discipline. Although the bombardment had minimal effect, tension in the garrison began to mount. One night, an artillery sentry in the south redoubt heard noises and, when his challenge went unanswered, fired a canister round into the darkness. The journal of Major Preston (actually written by Lieutenant John André, 7th Foot) records: "In the morning, a horse was found dead; this was the enemy our out sentry had seen and challeng'd." At left are Preston (1), André (2) and Samuel Mackay (3), commanding the Royal Highland Emigrant detachment. The first two are in regimental uniforms, whilst Mackay wears civilian clothing and a cut-down military coat of 1760s vintage (most Emigrants had no uniforms until late 1775 and wore a mix of everyday attire and old French and Indian War uniforms). Behind them are gunners of the Royal Regiment of Artillery, gathered around a 12-pdr field gun; the errant sentry (4) wears the distinctive white cartridge case and a powder horn for priming the gun. In the foreground are sergeants of the artillery (5) and the 26th Foot (6); the latter has left his cross-belts unwhitened, with the bayonet belt over the right shoulder, a practice becoming increasingly fashionable by 1775. Behind are a fifer of the 7th Foot (7) and a drummer of the 26th Foot (8).

Musicians of Royal regiments wore laced red coats faced blue, rather than the more usual reversed colors as worn by the drummer from the 26th. The fifer wears an old coat with the lace removed (probably to sew onto this year's coat). In well-managed regiments, the men retained old coats and hats for everyday duty to preserve new clothing. To the right of the musicians are a midshipman (9) and petty officer (10) from the naval contingent. The Royal Navy had no official uniforms for junior ranks at this time, but smaller vessels often issued matching clothing to their crews. On the parapet are two privates of the 26th Foot. The sentry (11) wears a watch coat (essentially a converted blanket) and watches for approaching shot and shell from enemy batteries, as well as troop movements. The workman (12) is repairing the parapet; even without enemy action, earthworks could be destroyed by the elements within two years, if not properly maintained. Below are an officer (13) and two men (14) of the Canadian (French-speaking) militia. Blue was the distinguishing color of the Montreal brigade, seen in the officer's sleeved waistcoat, and the men's "tunques" (wool bonnets). The women (15) are two of the almost 200 wives of enlisted men among the garrison; one has an officer's shirt to clean or mend, to supplement her husband's meager pay. Officially, a British infantry or artillery company took six wives overseas, but once on station, more were soon acquired from the local populace – a practice tolerated as long as the women behaved and assisted with nursing and domestic chores. (Adam Hook)

opportunity, Montgomery returned to St Johns that day with 2,000 men aboard a schooner, a sloop, two armed row galleys, and ten bateaux – sufficient to blockade both the fort and the river. He also had 40 Canadians recruited near Chambly by Livingston and Jeremy Duggan, a Quebec barber, and led by Major John Brown.

The Americans disembarked under sporadic artillery fire and encircled the fort. Brown captured a supply column from Laprairie and then occupied an old redoubt astride the road. The fort's commander, Major Charles Preston, sent out a patrol, which captured Hazen and forced Brown to abandon the work. Montgomery then arrived with 500 fresh troops and forced the British back to the fort with some loss but in good order. By the evening of 18 September the Americans had the fort surrounded and Preston sent Lorimier to inform Carleton of his predicament.

The next day, Montgomery sent patrols to warn of any relief attempt from Montreal – Brown went to Laprairie, while Allen (a subordinate any commander would happily send elsewhere) headed north with Livingston and Duggan to recruit more Canadians, and then occupied Longueuil. Few *habitants* took the bait. Local leaders, especially the clergy, made every effort to dissuade their neighbors from joining the Americans, and one group even wrote to Carleton, begging his pardon for not turning out with the militia. These loyalists expected immediate aid from Carleton, but he chose to remain in Montreal, which – though correct militarily – led many citizens to question the wisdom of openly backing the British. While few Canadians helped Livingston, none tried to hinder him and he was able to intercept all vessels coming up the Richelieu from Sorel.

Fort Chambly was a square stone structure with a bastion at each angle, but no outworks, and its thin masonry walls were proof only against musketry and smaller guns. Supposedly built to protect Montreal from British attack, it was probably intended as a supply depot for St Johns and to guard the portage around the nearby rapids. Brown and Easton showed that it was possible to bypass the fort and reach Montreal via Laprairie or Lachine, and then return to besiege it at leisure with no fear of relief arriving. (Author's photograph)

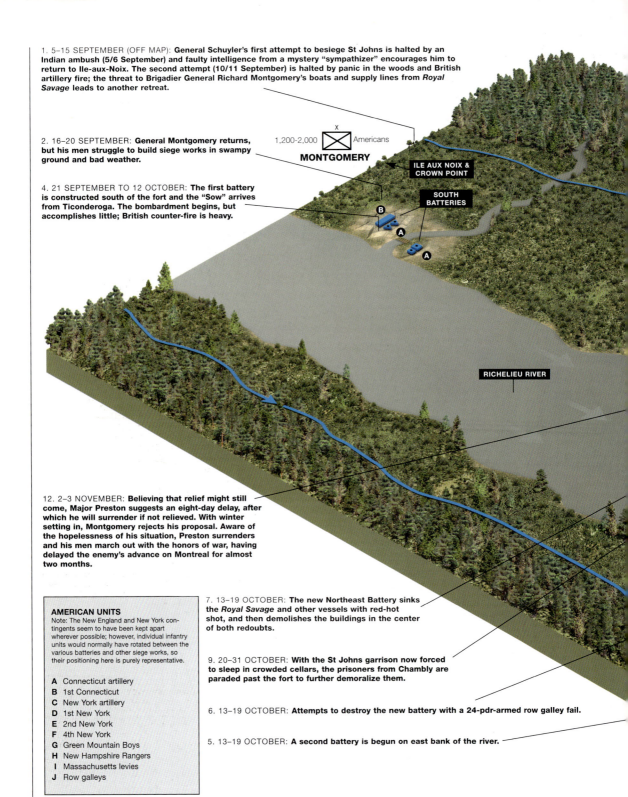

1. **5–15 SEPTEMBER (OFF MAP):** General Schuyler's first attempt to besiege St Johns is halted by an Indian ambush (5/6 September) and faulty intelligence from a mystery "sympathizer" encourages him to return to Ile-aux-Noix. The second attempt (10/11 September) is halted by panic in the woods and British artillery fire; the threat to Brigadier General Richard Montgomery's boats and supply lines from *Royal Savage* leads to another retreat.

2. **16–20 SEPTEMBER:** General Montgomery returns, but his men struggle to build siege works in swampy ground and bad weather.

4. **21 SEPTEMBER TO 12 OCTOBER:** The first battery is constructed south of the fort and the "Sow" arrives from Ticonderoga. The bombardment begins, but accomplishes little; British counter-fire is heavy.

1,200–2,000 X Americans

MONTGOMERY

ILE AUX NOIX & CROWN POINT

SOUTH BATTERIES

B

A

A

RICHELIEU RIVER

12. **2–3 NOVEMBER:** Believing that relief might still come, Major Preston suggests an eight-day delay, after which he will surrender if not relieved. With winter setting in, Montgomery rejects his proposal. Aware of the hopelessness of his situation, Preston surrenders and his men march out with the honors of war, having delayed the enemy's advance on Montreal for almost two months.

AMERICAN UNITS
Note: The New England and New York contingents seem to have been kept apart wherever possible; however, individual infantry units would normally have rotated between the various batteries and other siege works, so their positioning here is purely representative.

A Connecticut artillery
B 1st Connecticut
C New York artillery
D 1st New York
E 2nd New York
F 4th New York
G Green Mountain Boys
H New Hampshire Rangers
I Massachusetts levies
J Row galleys

7. **13–19 OCTOBER:** The new Northeast Battery sinks the *Royal Savage* and other vessels with red-hot shot, and then demolishes the buildings in the center of both redoubts.

9. **20–31 OCTOBER:** With the St Johns garrison now forced to sleep in crowded cellars, the prisoners from Chambly are paraded past the fort to further demoralize them.

6. **13–19 OCTOBER:** Attempts to destroy the new battery with a 24-pdr-armed row galley fail.

5. **13–19 OCTOBER:** A second battery is begun on east bank of the river.

THE SIEGE OF ST JOHNS

5 September to 3 November 1775, viewed from the northeast showing the gradually tightening noose the Americans cast around St Johns. Finally, with no realistic prospect of relief, Major Charles Preston has little choice but to surrender.

1. 1 NOVEMBER: **With the northeast battery now fully operational, St Johns receives its heaviest bombardment to date. Casualties are light, but valuable provisions and material are destroyed; Preston's officers inform him that there is food for only eight more days.**

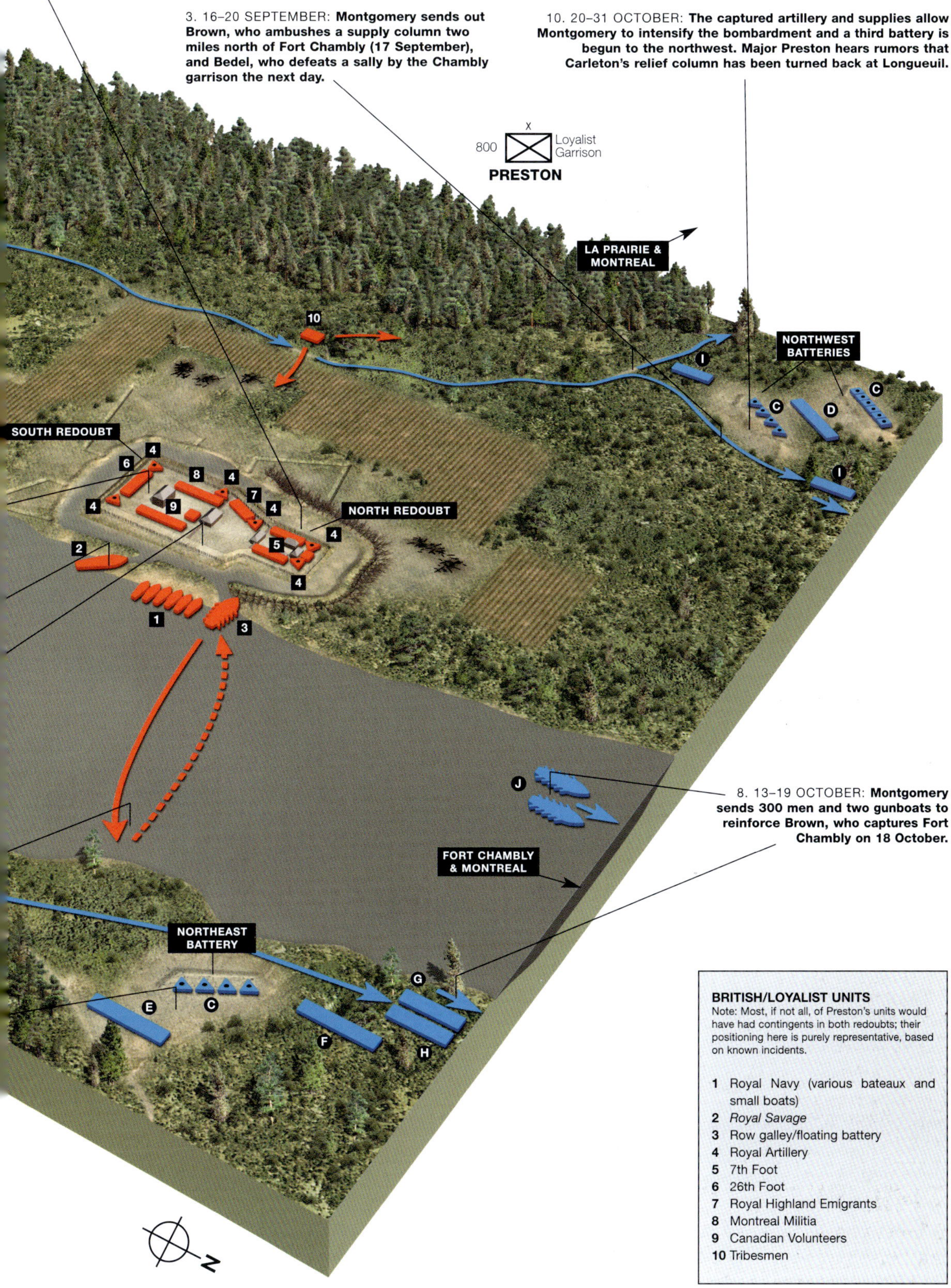

3. 16–20 SEPTEMBER: **Montgomery sends out Brown, who ambushes a supply column two miles north of Fort Chambly (17 September), and Bedel, who defeats a sally by the Chambly garrison the next day.**

10. 20–31 OCTOBER: **The captured artillery and supplies allow Montgomery to intensify the bombardment and a third battery is begun to the northwest. Major Preston hears rumors that Carleton's relief column has been turned back at Longueuil.**

x
800 ⊠ Loyalist Garrison
PRESTON

LA PRAIRIE & MONTREAL

10

NORTHWEST BATTERIES

I

C

C

D

C

SOUTH REDOUBT

4

6

8

4

7

4

I

4

9

4

5

NORTH REDOUBT

4

2

4

1

3

J

8. 13–19 OCTOBER: **Montgomery sends 300 men and two gunboats to reinforce Brown, who captures Fort Chambly on 18 October.**

FORT CHAMBLY & MONTREAL

NORTHEAST BATTERY

E

C

G

F

H

N

On 24 September, Allen and Brown met at Laprairie and hatched a plan to capture Montreal. The idea was presented by Allen, who was upset at losing command of the Green Mountain Boys to his cousin Seth Warner, and now had a commission but no command. Brown would cross from Laprairie and land south of the city with 200 men. Allen, with 30 men detached by Brown and 80 of his own (mostly Canadians), would cross from Longueuil and attack from the north. Allen ferried his men across during the night of 25 September and by dawn was awaiting the signal that Brown was ready. It never came.

Allen sent men to find Brown (who was still at Laprairie) and to obtain help from Thomas Walker inside the city. Walker tried to talk several fellow-citizens into unlocking the city gates, but by now a local man had spotted Allen and informed Carleton. Carleton, until now in despair of relieving St Johns because of the lack of support from the populace, found that a threat to Montreal itself produced a different response. While a few took their families down to the docks in order to escape, 120 French and 80 English volunteers armed themselves and reported for duty. They were joined by 34 men of the 26th Foot, six Indians, and 20 Indian Department officers, one of whom – Major John Campbell – took command of the force. As the British emerged, the Americans took cover in woods and buildings. Campbell placed his Regulars in the center and sent the volunteers to attack Allen's flanks, at which Duggan's recruits (on the right) panicked and fled. The men on Allen's left did the same, leaving Allen alone; 36 of his men were captured, five were killed, and ten wounded. Campbell lost two officers (including Major John Carden of the Legislative Council) and one soldier killed; a French *seigneur* and a Regular were wounded.

The victory saw over 1,200 militia flood in from the surrounding countryside, to add to the 600 in Montreal who, with Indians and Regulars, gave Carleton over 2,000 troops. Many now clamored to relieve St Johns. Instead, they remained in Montreal for four weeks until the militia drifted away for the harvest and to protect their homes from marauding bands of collaborators. The lack of action appeared culpable, but in truth Carleton had no firm intelligence on enemy numbers and location, and any of the American contingents roaming the countryside between Montreal and St

View of Montreal from the mountain, by James Peachey c.1784. The island measured about 30 miles by 12 (48 x 19km), within which two inlets of the St Lawrence formed a smaller island, three miles (4.8km) long and two-and-a-half (4km) wide, called the Isle de Jesus. The two mountains (the city's name was a corruption of Monts Royaux) offered uninterrupted views of the surrounding countryside, including the mountains at Chambly, and even as far as the Green Mountains east of Lake Champlain. (National Archives of Canada – C-002002)

Johns could easily have ambushed him. But if Carleton could not challenge Montgomery, he could improve security in Montreal and he issued a warrant for Walker's arrest. On 5 October, a detachment of Royal Highland Emigrants arrived at Walker's house. He fired on them, wounding two, and only surrendered when the soldiers set the house ablaze.

Back at St Johns, Montgomery had been delayed further by bad weather and by Preston's gunners, who had cleared a field of fire by leveling the buildings outside the fort. On 22 September, work began on the first battery, but with the besiegers outgunned by the defenders and by the vessels on the river, progress was slow. The American blockade was also extremely lax – Preston communicated regularly with Carleton and on 4 October, two Canadian officers rounded up eight cattle from nearby fields and brought them into the fort.

However, matters changed when heavier guns arrived from Fort Ticonderoga, including a large mortar immediately christened "the sow". By 15 October, the two buildings inside the fort were in ruins and, though casualties were negligible, the defenders were forced to sleep in the cellars. More worrying for Preston was a second American battery on the east bank, directly opposite the fort, which not only closed the route in for messengers and supplies, but also threatened the vessels moored there. Preston sent one of the row galleys, armed with a 24-pdr, to destroy the work, but after severe casualties on both sides it was forced to withdraw. The senior naval officer, Lieutenant William Hunter, now recommended that all three vessels be beached between the redoubts and their guns and stores removed. Before this task was completed, however, *Royal Savage* was holed by heated shot and sank with its ordnance still aboard, so infuriating Preston that Hunter had to defend his reputation in writing.

On 18 October, Preston suffered an even greater blow: Stopford surrendered the fort at Chambly, along with its garrison and valuable supplies of powder and shot. Brown and Livingston had surrounded the post with 400 men (half of them Canadian recruits) and had been joined later by Montgomery's two row galleys, which Duggan had slipped past

St Johns at night. After almost two days, the only damage was to the fort's chimneys, but this was enough to impress Stopford. While Chambly was not built to withstand a heavy bombardment, many cursed Stopford for not holding out longer and above all for not destroying the stores before surrendering. On 21 October, Preston and his men watched as the boats taking the Chambly garrison to prison camps in New England passed upriver. Such was the damage to the defenders' morale that the Canadian contingent petitioned Preston to let them surrender separately.

At Montreal, desertions among the militia (and the capture of a leading *seigneur* whilst recruiting replacements) had restricted Carleton to minor raids against Longueuil and Boucherville. Now he knew that time was running out for St Johns and he ordered MacLean to bring 180 troops down to Sorel from Quebec, and to recruit as many militia as he could on the way. By mid-October, with MacLean now leading 400 men, Carleton preparing to cross to Longueuil with 130 Regulars, 800 militia and 80 Indians and link up with MacLean just south of Chambly. Late in the afternoon of 30 October, Carleton's force set out in boats from St Helen's Island in the middle of the river. Immediately, they ran into musket fire from Seth Warner's 350 Green Mountain Boys and canister from two small cannon captured at Chambly. Unable to risk losing many men, Carleton withdrew, despite a successful landing by some Canadians and Conosadaga warriors farther downstream that could have been exploited. Just south of Sorel, MacLean learned of this setback while encountering strong opposition from Brown and Livingston and he too turned back.

As Carleton's men sat on St Helen's criticizing their commander's lack of aggression, Montgomery used two Canadian prisoners sent back by Warner to persuade Preston that further resistance was hopeless. The garrison was on salt rations and suffering from the lack of warmth and shelter, and the Americans – now numbering 2,000, excluding the detachments to the north – had completed another battery to the north-east. On 1 November, its guns opened fire, destroying vital supplies and causing serious damage to the defenses, though still not inflicting many casualties. That evening, Preston's officers announced that there was only enough food for eight more days, on two-thirds rations. At the same time, Montgomery wrote to Preston pointing out the human consequences of further bombardment, adding that if the fort was stormed, he would not be responsible for the consequences.

The following day, Preston sent an officer to negotiate terms. He attempted to paint an optimistic picture of the state of the garrison, but Montgomery sent him back with another letter, threatening to deny the honors of war and protection for the officers' possessions. Preston was for carrying on, but his officers were not. Terms were agreed on the evening of 2 November, although Preston demanded the removal of a clause expressing Montgomery's regret that the garrison's bravery had not been applied "in a better cause." On 3 November, 60 days after Schuyler's first attack, the garrison marched out with the honors of war, having lost 20 dead (half of whom were Indians or Canadians) and 23 wounded. Montgomery had suffered 100 combat casualties, but a further 1,000 men had been discharged due to illness. As he prepared to leave, Preston wrote a final insult to his captors in his journal: "We may thank our Enemy in some sort for leaving us in such slight field Works the credit of having been only reduced by Famine."

MONTGOMERY'S ADVANCE INTO CANADA

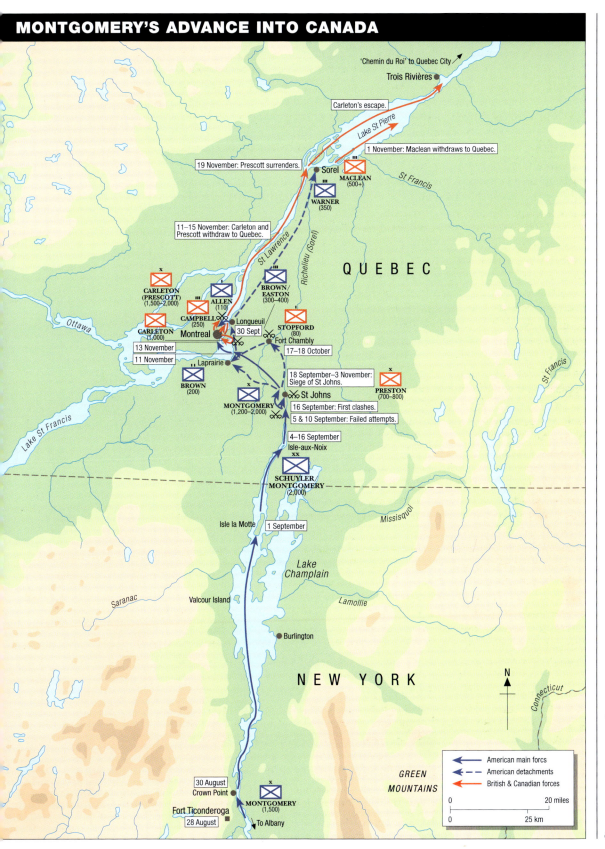

'Chemin du Roi' to Quebec City

Trois Rivières

Carleton's escape.

Lake St Pierre

1 November: Maclean withdraws to Quebec.

19 November: Prescott surrenders.

Sorel

MACLEAN (500+)

St Francis

WARNER (350)

11–15 November: Carleton and Prescott withdraw to Quebec.

St Lawrence

Richelieu (Sorel)

QUEBEC

CARLETON (PRESCOTT) (1,500–2,000)

ALLEN (110)

BROWN/ EASTON (300–400)

CAMPBELL (250)

Longueuil 30 Sept

STOPFORD (80)

CARLETON (1,000)

Montreal

Fort Chambly

17–18 October

Ottawa

13 November

11 November

Laprairie

18 September–3 November: Siege of St Johns.

PRESTON (700–800)

St Francis

BROWN (200)

MONTGOMERY (1,200–2,000)

St Johns

16 September: First clashes.

5 & 10 September: Failed attempts.

4–16 September

Isle-aux-Noix

SCHUYLER/ MONTGOMERY (2,000)

Lake St Francis

Missisquoi

Isle la Motte

1 September

Lake Champlain

Saranac

Valcour Island

Lamollie

Burlington

NEW YORK

N

Connecticut

30 August
Crown Point

GREEN MOUNTAINS

American main forcs

American detachments

British & Canadian forces

Fort Ticonderoga

MONTGOMERY (1,500)

28 August

To Albany

0   20 miles

0   25 km

MONTREAL

Carleton learned of the fall of St Johns on 4 November, by which time he also knew that more Americans were approaching Quebec through Maine. Nor would he receive the two regiments ordered from Boston in the summer. The commander of the North American squadron, Vice Admiral Samuel Graves, had refused to sail north so late in the year, even though vessels routinely docked safely in Quebec as late as November. Carleton wrote to Lord Dartmouth, Secretary of State for the Colonies, blaming the disaster on incompetence at Halifax and Boston, lack of support from the *habitants*, and traitors in Montreal. With Montgomery undoubtedly approaching, Carleton put the garrison and what stores he could save aboard a small flotilla, but – possibly from a sense of honor – did not set sail for Quebec until the American army was across the river.

Knowing that he must capture Montreal and Quebec before winter set in, Montgomery left St Johns without delay, sending Brown, Livingston and Easton to Sorel, to prevent Carleton escaping by boat. On arriving opposite Montreal on 11 November, he sent three men across to negotiate with the citizens. He was aware that the defenses were weak and the people demoralized, but saw benefits in magnanimity. Promising to allow every citizen "the peaceable enjoyment of their property of every kind," his troops entered the city on 13 November, taking over the barracks and public storehouses. Unfortunately, the pro-American citizens were not inclined to play the gracious victor. They demanded Montgomery listen only to them and treat the Loyalists as a conquered people. Their bitterness and Montgomery's decision to leave the loathsome David Wooster (and his equally troublesome Connecticut troops) in charge, would destroy relations with the Canadians and any hope of improving the level of support for the invaders.

Meanwhile, Carleton and Prescott had sailed for Quebec on 11 November, taking Thomas Walker with them. Guns had been spiked, and powder and ball thrown into the St Lawrence. Prescott had also suggested burning the barracks, but concerns for private property forced Carleton to deny the request. As the flotilla approached Sorel on 12 November, a vessel ran aground. By the time it was re-floated, the wind had dropped and the vessels had to anchor for three days. On 15 November, a flag of truce appeared, along with a letter signed by Easton demanding that the squadron surrender. To add substance, Brown rowed out to the ships and offered to show them a battery of 32-pdrs. An officer was sent ashore to confirm this, but either shirked his job or was hoodwinked by Brown (who had neither batteries, nor guns).

Carleton's flotilla mounted 30 guns, but again the threat of substantial loss of life made him hesitate. He called a council of war: one captain offered to attack the batteries while the rest headed for Quebec; another – a noted pilot, familiar with the dangerous waters around Sorel – offered to row him downriver. Carleton agreed to the latter proposal. Dressed as an *habitant*, he was spirited away, leaving Prescott with instructions to drop stores and heavy guns into the river, and then decide to surrender or risk passing the enemy positions. Prescott tried to negotiate with Easton, but the latter convinced him that his position was hopeless and on 19 November (the day Carleton reached Quebec) he surrendered along with 120 troops and almost 200 sailors. Aboard the captured fleet Easton found the guns Prescott had failed to destroy, as well as 200 pairs of shoes. He also discovered Thomas Walker, who immediately returned to Montreal to help Wooster pacify the city. Most importantly, Easton had acquired the ships Montgomery needed to transport his own men to Quebec.

As the first snows fell, Montgomery borrowed £5,000 from James Price to have winter clothing made from captured British uniforms, and weapons and ammunition manufactured at the Forges St Maurice. Leaving Livingston, now a colonel, to raise a regiment of Canadians, he set off for Quebec via Trois Rivières. Unfortunately, the men whose enlistments expired on 10 December now decided that their job – driving the Regulars and Papists back from the frontier – was done and headed for home, counting the journey as part of their service. With just 800 men, Montgomery wondered if he had the quantity, and quality, of troops to hold Montreal and take Quebec. Almost 200 miles (322km) away, Carleton had the same concerns about holding Quebec and retaking Montreal.

ARNOLD'S JOURNEY

THE MARCH THROUGH MAINE

Soon after the fall of Ticonderoga, Colonel Jonathan Brewer had submitted a plan for an attack on Quebec with 500 men via upper Massachusetts (modern-day Maine). Initially rejected, it was resurrected in July as a counterpoint to Schuyler's thrust up the Richelieu River. George Washington believed that, with insufficient troops to defend both Quebec and Montreal, Carleton would be forced to either abandon the Montreal area, or risk being defeated piecemeal.

The route followed two watercourses that ran almost continuously from the Atlantic to the St Lawrence and was familiar to the Abenaki and French missionaries. It had been mapped by the engineer Lieutenant John Montresor in 1761 and was believed by the British to be impassable to a large body of troops. However, many Americans disagreed, including Washington, who estimated it would take 20 days' march at worst. At a private meeting, he offered command of the expedition to Arnold, who accepted and immediately ordered 200 lightweight bateaux capable of carrying six or seven men and over 600lbs (270kg) of baggage and supplies. He also called for "active woodsmen, well acquainted with bateaux" and was inundated with volunteers. By 5 September, he had the 1,050 men required.

The first stage of the journey was an overland march to Newburyport, from where the force embarked for the Kennebec River. Precious time was wasted gathering supplies and clearing pay arrears and the advance party, under Captain Daniel Morgan, only set off on the three-day march to Newburyport on 11 September. It was 16 September before the force finally set sail. As the flotilla neared its destination heavy rain and thick fog caused several vessels to become lost or run aground among the scores of islands, but by 20 September all had arrived safely at Georgetown. Arnold ordered his flagship – the **Broad Bay** – to head up the Kennebec to Gardinerston where the bateaux were waiting. Built from pine boards nailed to oak ribs, they were up to 25ft (7.6m) long and weighed almost 450lbs (200kg), but had been built from green wood and were smaller than Arnold's specification. He had to order 20 more.

Four men were assigned to each bateau and Dr Senter noted their looks of apprehension at the state of the craft. The little army then moved to Fort Western, from where Arnold dispatched two reconnaissance parties to scout the first section of the route and on up to the frontier. He then divided his force into four groups which would march one day apart. The first, composed of the riflemen, was led by Morgan and would break the trail for the rest. The second, under Greene, comprised the companies of Captains Hubbard, Thayer, and Topham. Arnold initially chose Greene to lead the advance guard, but – true to form – the riflemen would only serve

Captain Daniel Morgan 1736–1802, by C.W. Peale. Morgan and Dearborn typified the excellent junior officers under Arnold's command. Morgan served in the French and Indian War, Pontiac's Rebellion, and Dunmore's War. In 1775, he raised a rifle company in Virginia and marched to Boston. Though not always sound in judgment, he was a natural leader – one of the few men able to control such troops. After his capture at Quebec, he was exchanged in the autumn of 1776. (Independence National Historical Park)

Captain Henry Dearborn 1751–1829, by C.W. Peale. A former medical student, Dearborn was a militia officer when war broke out and fought with distinction at Bunker Hill. On the march to Quebec, he fell ill and was left on the Chaudière River, but recovered in time to take part in the attack on 31 December. Unlike Morgan, he was not exchanged until March 1777. Unfortunately, his excellent service in the Revolution has been obscured by poor performances in the War of 1812. (Independence National Historical Park)

under Morgan. The third, commanded by Meigs, contained Dearborn's, Goodrich's, Hanchet's, and Ward's companies. The rearguard, under Enos, included those of McCobb, Scott, and Williams.

Arnold had estimated the distance to Quebec at 180 miles (290km); it was actually over 300 miles (480km). A mild taste of how much the terrain would exacerbate that underestimation occurred just half a mile (0.8km) beyond Fort Halifax, an abandoned outpost at the mouth of the Sebasticook River. The men had to hoist the bateaux out of the water, carry them along a thickly wooded bluff, then row upstream over five miles (8km) of rapids, before hoisting the bateaux and their contents up the 100ft (30m) rock face of the Skowhegan Falls. As they completed this task, an icy rain began to fall and the next morning their clothes were frozen. At Norridgewock, the last human habitation before the Chaudière, Arnold found Greene's command discarding spoiled food, leaving only salt pork and flour (both also in short supply). A growing number of men had dysentery and to make matters worse, the bateaux were capsizing as the green wood warped. Arnold had carpenters brought up from Gardinerston to make the necessary repairs, but it took almost a week and Arnold had to wait until 9 October before leaving Norridgewock.

However, at Carritunk Falls Morgan's men managed to kill a moose and catch trout to augment the rations and the following day saw further progress up the Kennebec River, now just a fast but shallow stream. By nightfall Arnold could see the mountain that marked the 12-mile (19km) "Great Carry" – a portage that avoided an impassable stretch of the Dead River just west of its junction with the Kennebec. The portage also included three large ponds that were quicker and easier to navigate than the meandering, tree-infested river. On 11 October, the first three divisions arrived at the first pond, where Arnold set up his headquarters. The following day one of Arnold's scouts, Lieutenant Steele, reported that one of his men had seen the sun shining on the Chaudière Pond, 15 miles (24km) distant, from a tree. Arnold ordered 20 axemen to clear the trail up as far as Sartigan, a former French outpost and the first human habitation on the Quebec side of the frontier. Goodrich's company built a storehouse to hold supplies for a possible retreat, and also a log hospital for the growing number of sick (now including men who had drunk the brackish water of the second pond).

On 16 October, the force reached the third pond, which had clean drinking water and from where the portage ran downhill for two miles (3.2km) to a small plain. This looked firm from a distance, but proved to be a swamp. The men stumbled through it until they reached another watercourse that brought them finally to the Dead. The river lived up to its name, running so still that the troops could hardly make out which way it flowed. It also meandered so much that the mountains to the north were behind the men as often as they were in front. That night Arnold bivouacked with Greene, whose men were now on half rations. Arnold sent Bigelow to collect food from the rear division and, while they were waiting, Meigs brought up two freshly butchered oxen.

The following day heavy rain prevented further progress for all but the advance party. As darkness fell, the fierce wind uprooted trees and forced the men to pitch their tents in clearings for safety. By the next morning the Dead River had risen over 8ft (2.4km), spoiling supplies,

drenching clothing and tents, and making it more difficult to follow the line of the river.

Arnold now had to decide whether to continue, or return to the Kennebec while enough food remained. He called a council of war at which all present agreed to continue. He then announced that he would go ahead to Sartigan and have supplies ferried back to the main body. Greene and Enos would retain only as many fit men as could be fed for 15 days and send everyone else back to Cambridge. The reduced force would, he argued, be able to reach Sartigan in two weeks. The next day 75 sick left by bateaux while Arnold headed for Sartigan in freezing rain. He pitched camp 20 miles (32km) from Chaudière Pond. When he awoke the next day two inches (5cm) of snow had fallen.

Several days after the meeting, Enos came to see Greene to discuss Arnold's plan. Enos felt that even providing enough food for just 30 men to continue would leave those returning with insufficient rations to reach the Kennebec; his officers had suggested that their entire division should return. Greene was dismayed, having assumed that only a handful of men from each division would return. Enos was for going on, but his own officers refused and he felt honor-bound to side with them.[5] He promised Greene four barrels of flour and two of pork for the onward journey, but when Greene sent officers to collect these, Enos's subordinates refused to hand over anything. Eventually Williams provided two barrels of flour. Arnold was just a few miles from the St Lawrence when word reached him that he now had little more than 650 men left.

Meanwhile, the advance party was approaching the frontier and the four-mile (6.4km) portage over Height of Land. Snow further hampered the two-mile (3.2km) uphill climb with the bateaux and the journey was only completed after nightfall. By dawn on 26 October they came to Seven Mile Stream (now Arnold River), where Steele again reported to Arnold, this time accompanied by a woodsman who confirmed that the local *habitants* were friendly. Arnold pressed on to Chaudière Pond after sending a message to the rest of the column to abandon any bateaux not being used to transport the sick. On the way he found a reconnaissance party under Captain Hanchet, marooned on an island, having waded over

View of the falls in the River Chaudière, by George Fisher. This view shows the perils that attended Arnold's force as it made its way along the river in small canoes and poorly manufactured bateaux. The figures in the foreground give some idea of the scale of this natural feature. (National Archives of Canada – C-041363)

two miles (3.2km) waist deep in the icy water. Another officer, Isaac Hull, was sent back to prevent the other divisions from making the same mistake.

On 27 October, Hanchet and his men set off for Sartigan on foot while Arnold continued by canoe taking Steele and six others with him. After 15 miles (24km) he reached some rapids where his five craft all capsized. Two bateaux were destroyed, weapons and ammunition lost, but nobody drowned. Lashing the remaining supplies to the three surviving craft, they set off again. At the last minute one of the party noticed that the river led to a lethal waterfall, and they portaged round it. The next day Arnold's own canoe sank and he was forced to join one of the two overcrowded bateaux. However, as darkness fell, he spotted the lights of Sartigan ahead.

Some way behind, Morgan's division was just crossing Height of Land. The men were now making soup from shoe leather and were so weak they struggled to climb the slope even without their bateaux. Several companies had already departed when Hull arrived. Dearborn set off to warn them using an abandoned canoe. Finding Goodrich, the two searched for a ford, sometimes wading up to their armpits, but without success, finding only one of Hanchet's men left behind as a punishment. The next day Dearborn began ferrying the men over the pond in the lone canoe, until Morgan, who had kept seven bateaux, arrived to help.

Meanwhile, Hull had become lost while leading Greene's division out of Seven Mile Stream. For two days they marched through the snow, covering 15 miles (24km) around the indented shoreline and occasionally following blind tributaries. Eventually they found footprints in the mud and followed them down to the Chaudière, passing the wreckage of Morgan's bateaux, which had suffered a similar fate to Arnold's, losing one man, the remaining flour, and Dr Senter's medical chest in the process. The men were now eating their belts and shoes, squirrel skins and Dearborn's Newfoundland dog. Many were also barefoot and their route

ew of Cape Diamond and the ains of Abraham, by George sher. This view overlooks the ute taken across the river Arnold's men in November, nd also the path Montgomery ok during the attack of 1 December. The causeway ong which he and his men dvanced was just 24ft (7.3m) ide, with a 300ft (91m) recipice on the landward side nd a steep drop down to the ver on the other. (National rchives of Canada – C-041361)

CARLETON (1,800)

Quebec

Point Levis
13 November

Pointe aux
Trembles
2 December

ARNOLD
(650)

9 November

Etchemin

Chaudiere

Trois Rivières

St Lawrence

La Beauce

Sartigan
2 November

MONTGOMERY
(300)

Sorel

Richelieu (Sorel)

28 November

31 October

Lake
Megantic

25 October

ENOS
300

*Lake
Moosehead*

WOOSTER
(500)

Montreal

Q U E B E C

P R O V I N C E

21 October

Flooded
area

19 October

Dead R.

Portage

16 October

20 November

Expired
enlistments
600

Lake
Champlain

Lake
Champlain

Norridgewock Falls
6–9 October

Androscoggin

25 September

Fort Western
(Augusta)

Gardiner
22 September

20 September

Kennebec

Connecticut

Lake
George

Hudson

NEW YORK

NEW
HAMPSHIRE

Portsmouth

19 September

Newburyport

ATLANTIC
OCEAN

11–13 September

MASSACHUSETTS

Cambridge

GAGE
(4,000)

5 September

Boston

ARNOLD
(1,050)

WASHINGTON
(20,000)

N

Legend:

- ⊠ British troops
- ⊠ Continental troops
- → Montresor's route (where different from Arnold's)
- → Arnold's route
- → Enos (and expired enlistments from Montreal)
- → Montgomery

0   25 miles
0   50 km

could be traced by the bloodstains in the snow. Men who fell or lagged behind were abandoned as the column snaked along the Chaudière for over 20 miles (32km). A private, retracing his route the following spring, found human bones scattered all along it. At noon on 2 November, a group of *habitants* delivered three head of cattle, and canoes arrived with mutton, flour, and oatmeal. By the next evening the troops were in Sartigan, where they were fed and housed, although Dearborn considered the hospitality of the *habitants* somewhat expensive.

Arnold summoned the local Indians. He promised that his men were there as liberators and, after defeating the British, they would go home and leave the red man in peace. Over 50 warriors enlisted on the spot and Arnold then set up his headquarters in the house of a *seigneur* who had been expelled for punishing anyone refusing to join the militia. Arnold next had a letter from George Washington to the people of Canada read out in the nearby church. Here he learned of the capture of St Johns in a letter from Montgomery. He immediately sent Meigs to find canoes, and a party of riflemen to reconnoiter the St Lawrence. By dawn on 8 November, the riflemen could see Quebec – and the two warships guarding the river.

THE SIEGE OF THE CITY

Unaware of Arnold's proximity, Cramahé was trying to keep control of the city. Militia patrolled the streets, the gates were shut at 6.00pm, and non-residents had to report to the guard commander. Like Carleton, he had no illusions about many habitants joining the garrison, though one British officer believed that this was more from opposition to the Quebec Act than support for the Americans. Nevertheless, known sympathizers such as McCord, Antill, Macaulay, and Mercier were all under surveillance, and many other merchants openly discussed surrender.

Reports of armed men at Point Lévis forced Cramahé to act. He warned off Macaulay, had Mercier confined on one of the warships, and arranged for all canoes and boats to be removed from the south bank of the river and Ile d'Orleans. On 3 November, the frigate *Lizard* arrived with money, militia uniforms, and 100 volunteers from Newfoundland. This raised spirits briefly, but five days later a landing party from the sloop *Hunter* was fired on by riflemen. On 12 November, MacLean returned from Sorel, having completed the journey by road after gales had forced him ashore. At last Cramahé, a lifelong civilian who was widely criticized but who had done much of value, had an officer he could entrust with the defense of the city. The garrison now comprised 1,126 men. More importantly they were led by officers such as captains John Nairne, Malcolm Frazer, and George Laws of MacLean's own regiment, militia colonels Henry Caldwell and Noël Voyer, and Captain John Hamilton of the Royal Navy – men who could be depended on in a crisis.

By 13 November, Arnold had acquired 40 canoes and at 9.00pm the first wave set off. Passing between *Lizard* and *Hunter* and eluding the patrolling guard boats, they landed a mile (1.6km) above Wolfe's Cove. As the canoes returned for a second trip, the first group occupied a house and lit a fire. They were spotted immediately and shots were exchanged. Despite the loss of surprise, by 4.00am three waves with over

500 men had crossed safely. The remainder followed over the next few days, leaving Hanchet and 50 men to guard Point Lévis. Arnold followed Wolfe's path onto the Plains of Abraham and called a council of war to discuss whether to storm the city that night. Morgan was in favor but, with over 100 men and most of the scaling ladders still on the south bank, he was outvoted.[6]

Morgan then occupied the suburb of St Foy, seizing large quantities of cattle and potatoes and looting houses. While the men were eating, one of Morgan's sentries was captured by a British patrol. This suggested a level of boldness on the part of the enemy that Arnold believed he could use to his advantage. Intending to provoke an attack, Arnold formed up his men in front of the city walls (now swarming with troops) and gave three cheers. Some shots were exchanged and a few of Morgan's riflemen moved out in front of the line to snipe at the spectators, but to no avail. Febiger even walked to within 100yds (90m) of the wall, but returned without a scratch. MacLean promptly ordered the buildings near the Porte St Jean to be burned, to deny cover to the riflemen.

Arnold then wrote to Cramahé, offering to spare private property if he surrendered. It took two attempts to deliver the letter, the officer chosen being forced to take cover from cannon fire despite being under a flag of truce. On 16 November, Cramahé called a council of war, at which MacLean announced that the garrison now numbered 1,178, that the 5,000 civilians already had enough food to last until spring, and that food and firewood were still coming in through the American lines. Not surprisingly, the vote was unanimous in favor of holding out.

Two days later, Arnold learned that MacLean was planning a sortie. An inventory of his own military supplies revealed that over 100 muskets had been irreparably damaged and that his musket men had less than five rounds each. Even Morgan, with whom Arnold had quarreled the previous day over rations, agreed that the only option was to retreat 20 miles (32km) to Pointe aux Trembles and await the arrival of Montgomery. By dawn the next day, the troops pulled back through the villages along the north bank of the river and Hanchet abandoned Point Lévis.

View of Quebec from the south-east, by Joseph Des Barres. The routes taken by Montgomery and Arnold can be clearly seen at the extreme left and right of the lower town (the center of which was the intended *rendezvous* point). The governor's house stands on the eminence in the center of the upper town (just to the right of the ship) and was thought safe from enemy bombardment until ball passed through a room next to where his family were playing cards. (National Archives of Canada – C-0041377)

At Pointe aux Trembles the men enjoyed home comforts while Arnold ordered shirts, stockings, caps and mittens, ammunition, rum, and money from Montreal. Whilst awaiting Montgomery, Arnold experienced the first signs of discontent with his style of leadership. When Arnold ordered Hanchet to transport cannon to Sillery by bateaux he refused. Later in the siege, several captains would ask Montgomery to transfer them from Arnold's command.

On 2 December, a schooner and two smaller vessels, both loaded with Montgomery's troops, arrived at Point aux Trembles. The combined force returned to Quebec, Montgomery setting up his headquarters in St Foy. With his New Yorkers occupying the Plains of Abraham, he sent Arnold's musket men to St Roche and the riflemen to the meadows along the St Charles River. He then had a message to the merchants shot into the city with arrows and used a local woman to deliver an ultimatum to Carleton. Carleton read the document, ordered a servant to put it in the fire and had the old woman put in jail and later drummed out of the city.

Carleton now assigned his Regulars, Marines, and Emigrants to MacLean, and the sailors to Captain John Hamilton of the Royal Navy. Colonel Henry Caldwell took command of the British militia and Noël Voyer the French, while the engineer, James Thompson, had blockhouses, gun platforms and barricades built to cover the main streets of the Lower Town. Meanwhile, Montgomery began the bombardment of the city from a battery of five mortars in St Roche, but two days of shelling produced few casualties and merely improved the confidence of the civilian population. Much more damaging were the efforts of the riflemen, who began picking off defenders on the ramparts. However, the dangers were not one-sided – cannon on the walls made it dangerous for the Americans to show themselves. One shell destroyed Montgomery's sleigh, killing his horse, while he was conferring with his officers.

Montgomery ordered a new battery constructed closer to the walls and Lamb selected a site some 700yds (640m) from the Porte St Jean, behind some houses. With the earth frozen digging was out of the

Guardroom of the Dauphine Bastion. Part of the 18th-century defenses, this was where Dearborn and some of his men were held immediately after their capture. The city walls were generally 25ft (7.6m) thick and over 20ft (6m) high, although problems with the foundations due to the freezing of the ground in winter, had created irregularities in some places. (Author's photograph)

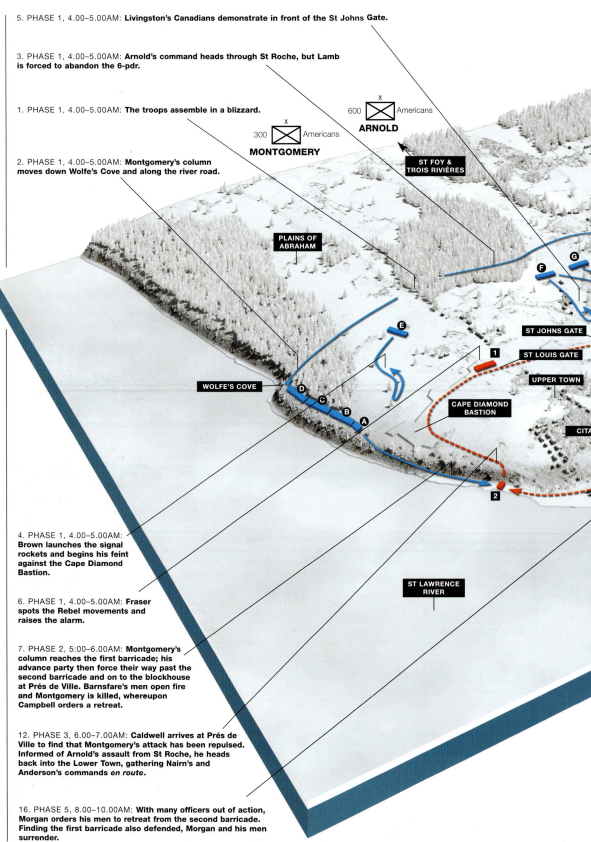

5. **PHASE 1, 4.00–5.00AM: Livingston's Canadians demonstrate in front of the St Johns Gate.**

3. **PHASE 1, 4.00–5.00AM: Arnold's command heads through St Roche, but Lamb is forced to abandon the 6-pdr.**

1. **PHASE 1, 4.00–5.00AM: The troops assemble in a blizzard.**

2. **PHASE 1, 4.00–5.00AM: Montgomery's column moves down Wolfe's Cove and along the river road.**

4. **PHASE 1, 4.00–5.00AM: Brown launches the signal rockets and begins his feint against the Cape Diamond Bastion.**

6. **PHASE 1, 4.00–5.00AM: Fraser spots the Rebel movements and raises the alarm.**

7. **PHASE 2, 5:00–6.00AM: Montgomery's column reaches the first barricade; his advance party then force their way past the second barricade and on to the blockhouse at Prés de Ville. Barnsfare's men open fire and Montgomery is killed, whereupon Campbell orders a retreat.**

12. **PHASE 3, 6.00–7.00AM: Caldwell arrives at Prés de Ville to find that Montgomery's attack has been repulsed. Informed of Arnold's assault from St Roche, he heads back into the Lower Town, gathering Nairn's and Anderson's commands *en route*.**

16. **PHASE 5, 8.00–10.00AM: With many officers out of action, Morgan orders his men to retreat from the second barricade. Finding the first barricade also defended, Morgan and his men surrender.**

600 Americans
x
ARNOLD

300 Americans
x
MONTGOMERY

ST FOY & TROIS RIVIÉRES

PLAINS OF ABRAHAM

E

D
C
B
A

WOLFE'S COVE

F
G

ST JOHNS GATE

ST LOUIS GATE

1

UPPER TOWN

CAPE DIAMOND BASTION

CITADE

2

ST LAWRENCE RIVER

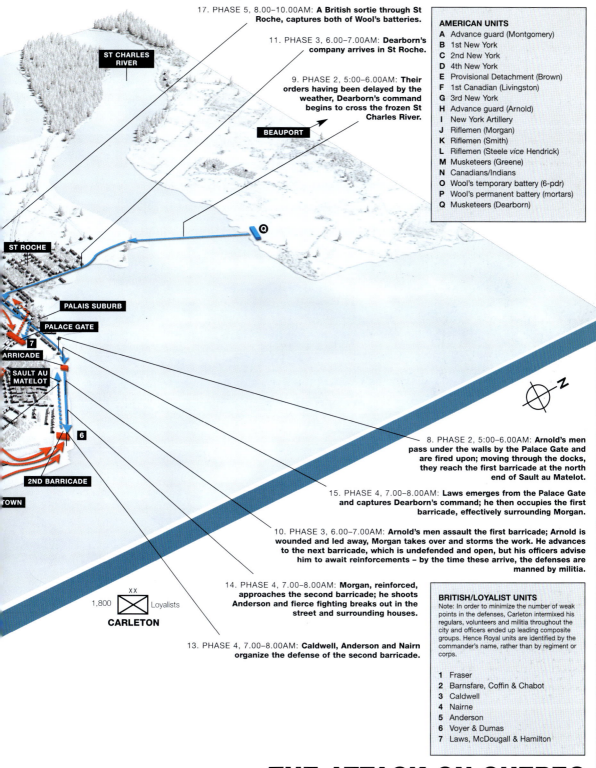

17. PHASE 5, 8.00–10.00AM: A British sortie through St Roche, captures both of Wool's batteries.

11. PHASE 3, 6.00–7.00AM: Dearborn's company arrives in St Roche.

9. PHASE 2, 5:00–6.00AM: Their orders having been delayed by the weather, Dearborn's command begins to cross the frozen St Charles River.

ST CHARLES RIVER

BEAUPORT

ST ROCHE

PALAIS SUBURB

PALACE GATE

7

ARRICADE

SAULT AU MATELOT

6

2ND BARRICADE

OWN

AMERICAN UNITS

A Advance guard (Montgomery)
B 1st New York
C 2nd New York
D 4th New York
E Provisional Detachment (Brown)
F 1st Canadian (Livingston)
G 3rd New York
H Advance guard (Arnold)
I New York Artillery
J Riflemen (Morgan)
K Riflemen (Smith)
L Riflemen (Steele *vice* Hendrick)
M Musketeers (Greene)
N Canadians/Indians
O Wool's temporary battery (6-pdr)
P Wool's permanent battery (mortars)
Q Musketeers (Dearborn)

8. PHASE 2, 5:00–6.00AM: Arnold's men pass under the walls by the Palace Gate and are fired upon; moving through the docks, they reach the first barricade at the north end of Sault au Matelot.

15. PHASE 4, 7.00–8.00AM: Laws emerges from the Palace Gate and captures Dearborn's command; he then occupies the first barricade, effectively surrounding Morgan.

10. PHASE 3, 6.00–7.00AM: Arnold's men assault the first barricade; Arnold is wounded and led away, Morgan takes over and storms the work. He advances to the next barricade, which is undefended and open, but his officers advise him to await reinforcements – by the time these arrive, the defenses are manned by militia.

14. PHASE 4, 7.00–8.00AM: Morgan, reinforced, approaches the second barricade; he shoots Anderson and fierce fighting breaks out in the street and surrounding houses.

1,800   X X   Loyalists

CARLETON

13. PHASE 4, 7.00–8.00AM: Caldwell, Anderson and Nairn organize the defense of the second barricade.

BRITISH/LOYALIST UNITS
Note: In order to minimize the number of weak points in the defenses, Carleton intermixed his regulars, volunteers and militia throughout the city and officers ended up leading composite groups. Hence Royal units are identified by the commander's name, rather than by regiment or corps.

1 Fraser
2 Barnsfare, Coffin & Chabot
3 Caldwell
4 Nairne
5 Anderson
6 Voyer & Dumas
7 Laws, McDougall & Hamilton

THE ATTACK ON QUEBEC

31 December 1775, 4.00am–10.00am, viewed from the southeast, showing Montgomery's and Arnold's disastrous attempt to seize the city, which results in Montgomery's death and the capture of Captain Daniel Morgan and his men.

question, so the gunners filled their gabions with snow and doused them with water to create walls of ice. The battery was finished in three nights and was soon the target of British fire, but the results were not visible as the houses were in the way. Carleton ordered them demolished, but his gunners set them ablaze instead and a strong wind almost carried the fire into the city. A few days later, he refused demands from his officers to burn St Foy and St Roche.

However, with the houses gone, Lamb's battery was exposed and quickly destroyed – two guns were knocked out, three men killed and several others wounded. On the night of 17 December, the guns were removed, and the following day Montgomery made one last effort to coax Carleton into surrendering. Arnold delivered a letter promising Carleton and Cramahé safe passage to England, but was kept waiting outside the gates until one of Carleton's aides announced from the walls that the governor would neither read the letter nor treat with rebels.

Montgomery was now being urged to storm the city without further delay (although rumors that he already had were sweeping England and North America). His Canadians wanted action and the enlistments of many American soldiers would expire on 31 December. He wrote to David Wooster and George Washington, outlining the difficulties and promising to attack at the first heavy snowstorm, relying on the garrison being spread thinly around the city whilst concentrating his own forces. On Christmas Day, he told the army of his plan. Most of the troops supported it and he received a rousing cheer, heard on the ramparts, but a significant number admitted to being apprehensive or downright skeptical. On 27 December, a snowstorm blew up, lasting all day and into the night. The troops made ready – the New Yorkers and four musket companies from Arnold's contingent would attack the Cape Diamond Bastion, whilst Greene would lead the rest into the Lower Town. However, just after midnight the wind died, the sky cleared, and the attack was cancelled – fortuitously as it turned out, as a prisoner and a deserter had escaped and warned Carleton. Montgomery changed his plan, but now had another problem to deal with – smallpox. A second hospital was established three miles (5km) away, but it was soon overflowing and, despite orders to the contrary, many men inoculated themselves.

On the afternoon of 30 December, another storm blew up. By nightfall it had become the heavy "northeaster" Montgomery desired and around 4.00am he ordered the troops to form up. He would lead 300 New Yorkers past Cape Diamond and into the Lower Town from the south. Arnold, with 600 men including 50 gunners, would leave St Roche and attack from the north through the Sault au Matelot. At the same time Livingston would feint against the Porte St Jean with his Canadians, and Brown would engage the Cape Diamond bastion with 100 men. Montgomery and Arnold would join forces and head into the Upper Town, hoping the merchants would panic and force Carleton to surrender. In fact, Carleton had issued orders to burn the wharves and warehouses in such an event.

As Brown released the signal rockets to start the operation, Montgomery led his column down to Wolfe's Cove, where they headed east, negotiating large blocks of ice and climbing the rocky precipice on the landward side wherever the river bank was blocked. As they neared Prés de Ville they heard the bell of Notre Dame des Victoires over the

Captain James Wilkinson 1757–1825, by C.W. Peale. As villains of the Revolution, Wilkinson and Burr barely rank below Arnold (post-betrayal) and are remarkable only for their ability to survive some highly dubious acts. Yet strangely both showed considerable fortitude and bravery during Arnold's expedition and the attack on Quebec. Wilkinson was born in Maryland, studied medicine, and joined Thompson's Pennsylvania rifle battalion on the outbreak of war. He befriended Burr on the march through Maine and, after being promoted to captain, replaced Burr as Arnold's *aide-de-camp*. After the war, he and Burr attempted to establish a separate nation along the Mississippi, but Wilkinson betrayed Burr and escaped unscathed. (Independence National Historical Park)

wind rousing the city. Sentries had spotted lanterns bobbing about in the swirling snow and the citizens were arming themselves.

Below the tip of Cape Diamond the column was stopped by a line of picket posts running from the river's edge to the cliff. Four were cut down and Montgomery stepped through the gap and walked to the next barrier. Taking a saw, he cut through two posts beside the cliff (to avoid enemy lines of fire) and slipped through, accompanied by a dozen officers and men. After a brief conference with his aides, Montgomery unsheathed his sword, held it aloft and led the advance across the open space between the barricade and a two-story blockhouse. The building held four small cannon manned by nine sailors and some 30 French and nine British militiamen. When the advancing Americans were about 50yds (45m) away they opened fire. Montgomery was hit in the head and killed instantly. So too were his aides, Captains Jacob Cheesemen and John Macpherson, a sergeant, and most of the men with him.

Montgomery's deputy quartermaster, Colonel Donald Campbell, was now the senior officer. Moving forward he found about 50 men at the second barricade, their muskets useless in the snowstorm. The surviving officers recommended withdrawal and Campbell agreed, taking command of the rearguard as the column fell back along the riverbank. Inside the blockhouse the occupants apparently panicked, having no idea what was happening outside. Later when news of Arnold's attack arrived, a Boston loyalist, John Coffin, used his bayonet to stop the men abandoning the post.

On the other side of the city, Arnold's column was led by 30 riflemen and Lamb's gunners with a brass 6-pdr on a sled. Behind them were the remaining riflemen, under Morgan, Steele, and Hendricks. Then came Greene's and Meigs' contingents, and finally the Indians and Canadians. A message had been sent to Dearborn on the north bank of the St Charles, but he had not shown up. Arnold could only hope he would join en route.

As the rockets went off, they moved through St Roche. Opposite the Porte Palais the main body was spotted by sentries and the whole column was struck by musketry and grenades from the ramparts. Lamb's 6-pdr was abandoned after becoming stuck in a snowdrift and the gunners became infantrymen. As the column passed through the docks it reached the first barrier across Sault au Matelot, defended by 30 militia and three cannon. Without Lamb's gun, Arnold had no option but to launch a frontal assault.

As the column surged forward, Arnold was struck in the left ankle by a ricocheting bullet. A rifleman and Chaplain Spring carried him back to Dr Senter. Almost instinctively the men turned to Morgan, who responded by leading them forward and being the first to scale a ladder. Musket fire scorched his face, knocking him off the ladder, but he climbed back up again with two riflemen, jumped onto the gun platform and rolled under one of the cannon to avoid the bayonets of the defenders. His men followed up the ladder and within minutes had captured the 30 defenders for the loss of one dead and six wounded.

Morgan then raced up Sault au Matelot to the next barricade. Finding the gate open and unguarded, he surveyed the work and returned. However, his officers refused to push on until the main body came up, fearing that their growing haul of prisoners (three times their

BENEDICT ARNOLD IS WOUNDED DURING THE ATTACK ON QUEBEC CITY, 31 DECEMBER 1775 (pages 58–59)

The northern force, under Benedict Arnold, comprised an advance guard of 30 men, led by Arnold in person, accompanied by a 6-pdr field piece lashed to a sled. This group was followed by three companies of riflemen, then two companies of musketeers, with 50 Canadian volunteers and several Indians bringing up the rear. As Arnold led his men through the St Roche suburb and into a narrow street called "Sault au Matelot" they were confronted by a barricade manned by 30 or 40 Canadian militia and three small cannon (1). The original plan was to bombard any fortifications with the 6-pdr, but this had become stuck in a snowdrift and had been abandoned. Without artillery support, Arnold (2) had to make a frontal assault, but while leading his men forward, he was shot in the left leg and was carried off by Chaplain Spring (3) and a rifleman (4), shouting encouragement to his men as he withdrew. At this point, Morgan (5) arrived and Arnold's men turned to him almost automatically for leadership. He immediately led an attack on the barricade, forcing aside a rifleman who was hesitating at the base of the first scaling ladder. As Morgan mounted the barricade, several muskets went off close to his face, scorching him and knocking him from the ladder. Undaunted, he climbed back up the ladder, accompanied by

two riflemen – Charles Porterfield (6) and William Heth (7). Clearing the barricade, he jumped onto a gun platform, rolling under the gun to avoid the bayonets thrust at him by the defenders. Inspired by his example, his men followed him over the defenses, capturing 30 militia and several civilians. Unfortunately, whilst attacking another barricade (which Morgan had previously reconnoitered alone and found unguarded) the entire force became trapped in the narrow streets and had to surrender after suffering heavy losses. Arnold's men (described by one observer as "famine-proof veterans" after their march through the Maine wilderness) had scraps of paper in their hats as a field sign, those who could write scribbling "Liberty or Death" on the paper. Most had overcoats made from captured blankets and some wore British uniforms, replacing the clothing lost or destroyed on the march to Quebec. Contemporary accounts suggest that Arnold may have been wearing a "blanket coat" over the uniform of a captain in the Governor's Foot Guards of Connecticut. On their way into the city, Arnold's men had encountered knee-deep snowdrifts; in the narrow streets the snow was piled up against the walls of the houses (many could only be entered through windows on the upper floor), but was only ankle-deep in the roadways, which had been kept clear by the garrison. (Adam Hook)

own number) would overpower any guards. It was another 30 minutes before the main body caught up and the delay would prove fatal. Still further back, Dearborn's company, delayed by a high tide, was only just entering St Roche.

Meanwhile, Caldwell, with a detachment of British Militia, was investigating the activity at Cape Diamond. Spotting Brown's action as a feint, he was returning to report to Carleton when he learned of Arnold's attack on Sault au Matelot. Picking up 30 Royal Highland Emigrants under Captain John Nairne of MacLean's regiment and 50 sailors led by a former naval officer named Anderson, he headed for the second barricade. There he found 200 French Militia under Voyer and Captain Alexandre Dumas, and a company of the 7th Foot, all in a state of confusion not knowing how to defend the barricade. Dispersing the militia and Emigrants into the surrounding houses, he formed the Regulars in a double line behind the 12ft (3.6m) high barricade, with cannon mounted on a platform immediately behind them pointing down the Sault au Matelot.

Reinforced by the Pennsylvanian riflemen, and Greene's and Meigs' detachments, Morgan led his men toward the second barricade. Some sailors, led by Anderson, sallied through the gate and blocked his path. Anderson called on Morgan to surrender, at which Morgan shot him dead and the sailors retreated through the gate. Shouting "Quebec is ours!" Morgan's men surged forward, but were caught in a hail of musketry from the upper windows of the houses. With men falling on every side, the Americans placed their ladders against the barricade but were beaten back. Some riflemen tried to outflank the barricade through a house, but were cleared out at bayonet point by Nairne. At this point the Americans could still have escaped, but as Steele, Topham, Hendrick, and Lamb all fell wounded, Morgan ordered his men into the houses. Once inside, they refused to venture out into the hail of lead.

Informed of events in Sault au Matelot, Carleton ordered Captain George Laws to retake the first barricade with 500 Emigrants and sailors. Laws emerged from the Porte Palais only to encounter Dearborn still blundering around St Roche. With their powder damp, Dearborn's men could not fight back and his entire group was captured and taken into the Upper Town. Laws then continued toward the first barricade, but found himself entirely alone amongst Morgan's men. He tried to bluff them into surrendering but was taken prisoner. However, once his men re-occupied the barricade the Americans' fate was sealed. After holding out until 10.00am, one group after another gave up as they ran out of ammunition. Finally, only Morgan was left. Refusing to surrender to a British officer, he handed his sword to a priest.

Carleton ordered a small force to deal with Wool's battery in St Roche. Wool was reinforced by men of the 3rd New York and Livingston's Canadians, but the British managed to capture the guns and withdraw successfully. Beyond that, however, Carleton would not risk his men outside the city walls – a decision that was not unanimously supported. Caldwell, in particular, suggested that more aggression would have finished the Americans off. Nonetheless, the moment of crisis had passed.

Back at Camp, Arnold wrote to David Wooster confirming the defeat and Montgomery's death and begging Wooster to relieve him. At one point, fearing a sortie by the garrison, he issued muskets to the patients in the hospital. Of his own command, at least 30 were dead (20 more bodies were found after the spring thaw and several reportedly fell through the ice while fleeing across the frozen rivers) and 42 wounded, the latter being among the 426 prisoners now under guard in Quebec. Another dozen had been slain alongside Montgomery. Carleton had lost six dead (Anderson and five militia privates) and one militiaman wounded.

Montgomery's body was found the next day and given a quiet but decent burial on 5 January, along with Macpherson and Cheeseman. Two days after the attack, Meigs was allowed out on parole to collect the personal belongings of those captured and bring them into the city. With 100 men leaving as their enlistments expired, Arnold now had barely 600 fit men. Wooster would not leave Montreal, however, as, with only 600 men himself, he feared the defeat would inspire an uprising. He sent Antill and Hazen to Albany to tell Schuyler, who, though shocked, could send no reinforcements as the enlistments of his own men were about to expire, and he needed the rest to oppose Johnson, who was rallying Indians and Loyalists in the Mohawk Valley. General Washington was equally powerless to help, as the refusal of Congress to authorize long-term enlistments (or even to offer bounties for re-enlistment) had left his own army short of men. New Hampshire, Massachusetts, and Connecticut were asked to raise one regiment each specifically for service in Canada. However, even these colonies were struggling to find recruits; those that could, refused to allow their men to serve in "mixed" units. At this point, Washington considered resigning.

---

5 When Enos returned to Cambridge, he was court-martialed, but fortunately had only his own officers as witnesses, and was acquitted with honor. Three of the court – Sullivan, Stark, and Brewer – believed Enos saved the rest by returning.

6 It later transpired that one of the city gates was unlocked and only lightly guarded.

THE RETREAT

CRISIS AT QUEBEC

The winter of 1775 was one of the worst in living memory. Outnumbered almost three to one, the best Arnold could do now was to deny the enemy firewood and forage, so he systematically burned outlying buildings and even some of the ships moored in the river. Carleton remained inside the city and refused to discuss prisoner exchanges, which Arnold sought to regain his only experienced artillery officer, Lamb.

From late January, American reinforcements began arriving from Ticonderoga via Montreal, including Warner's Green Mountain Boys and the first units from New Jersey and Pennsylvania. However, the journey had left the men in poor health, their uniforms in tatters and their weapons unserviceable. They arrived to find the camp riddled with smallpox (allegedly started by a prostitute sent out by Carleton), so much so that the other sick and the wounded were denied attention. Dr Senter reported 400 smallpox cases, mostly among the New Englanders; apparently, half of Warner's and Brown's men had disobeyed orders and inoculated themselves.

Equally worrying was the lack of specie. On 4 March, Arnold proclaimed that whoever accepted paper money would be paid in full, in coin, within four months. The ruse kept the army supplied for a few more months, but stories of troops looting from civilians – even priests and nuns – at bayonet point became rife. Discipline was collapsing and men overheard talking of going home when their enlistments expired were flogged. Even among officers morale was low, a situation not helped by the campaign still being waged against Arnold by Brown, Easton, and others.

The effect was to cause the *habitants* to reconsider their loyalties. On 23 March, 300 assembled to attack a detachment of Arnold's troops at Point Lévis. Arnold learned of this and sent Major Lewis Dubois with 150 New Yorkers to the south shore, where they were joined by 150 rebel Canadians. Dubois dispersed the 46-strong advance party, killing three and wounding several more. Soon after, Carleton's sentries noticed men erecting a battery at Point Lévis. Despite constant shelling, the battery became operational on 2 April, throwing red-hot shot at the town and the shipping in the river. Later that day, three men, believed to be Wooster, Arnold, and Antill, were seen surveying the town from a distance of 500 yards (457m). The next day, a second battery sprouted in front of Porte St Louis; a third later appeared across the St Charles.

The lack of trained artillerymen meant that Arnold could never match the weight and number (148) of Carleton's guns, but even so the governor took no chances. When a foraging party found recently manufactured scaling ladders outside the St Louis Bastion, he ordered the snow drifts cleared from the ditch, barricaded the Lower Town with blocks of ice from the river, built two blockhouses outside the walls, and cut a trench in the river ice under Cape Diamond to prevent the picket barriers being outflanked. At night, fireballs lit the darker recesses of the ditch. But the attack never came.

Although no attack came from the outside, the prisoners inside the city were active. The officers in the upper floor of the Seminary, and the enlisted men housed in the Récollet Monastery, and later the Dauphine Bastion, prepared to escape, but both attempts were thwarted. However, some did find a way out. The Royal Highland Emigrants had recruited 94 men from among the British-born prisoners, who were guilty of treason and therefore liable to hang. Within days, 14 of them had gone over the wall (literally) and Carleton had the rest disarmed. Otherwise, American activity was reduced to indiscriminate shelling of the Upper and Lower Towns – an act condemned by many of the captured officers watching the bombardment from the windows of the Seminary.

On 1 May, Major General John Thomas of Massachusetts replaced Wooster, bringing with him over 1,200 men. On the night of 3 May, with the river now open, a brig was spotted moving upriver. However, when it failed to answer the identification signals Carleton had agreed with Pringle before his departure, the guns in the Lower Town pounded the vessel. Men were seen fleeing in a small boat: the brig was a fireship designed to destroy the shipping at Queen's Wharf. It was also the swansong of the American forces besieging Quebec.

Concerned at the state of the army, Thomas had proposed to withdraw to Jacques Cartier and Deschambault and fortify those places. Unfortunately, the following day saw the arrival of the first British ships – the frigate *Surprise* closely followed by the ship *Isis* and the sloop *Martin*. From them disembarked 200 men of the 29th Foot and Marines. Learning that Thomas was pulling back, Carleton immediately ordered a sortie. Adding the 7th Foot, Royal Highland Emigrants, and city militia to the fresh troops, he attacked Thomas's encampment with 900 men and turned the latter's orderly withdrawal into a panic-stricken retreat.

By 7 May the exhausted Americans – many with smallpox – had halted in Deschambault, where they were shelled by British vessels on the St Lawrence. Thomas wanted to make a stand but his army did not. The men were tired and sick and the position could easily be taken in the rear by Carleton, who had complete command of the river. Thomas ordered his troops back to Sorel, leaving 500 men to garrison Deschambault, but even these were withdrawn several days later.

MISMANAGEMENT AT MONTREAL

Despite events at Quebec, the beginning of 1776 saw Congress still sanguine that French Canadians would not only welcome "liberation" but would actively support it. While the recruiting parties for Livingston's and Hazen's new regiments had barely scraped together 500 recruits, the *habitants* were still providing supplies (at a price) and refusing to help Carleton. As long as the Americans behaved reasonably, the worst that could happen was that the people stayed passive.

As an Irishman, Montgomery, like Carleton, was aware of Catholic sensitivities, and had noted the *habitants'* disregard for the clergy when

Charles Carroll 1737–1832, by C.W. Peale after R. Peale. Carro[ll] was born in Maryland and studied in France before practicing law in London. His support for independence saw him appointed to Congress and although his Catholicism barred him from public and professiona[l] life in Maryland, it made him an obvious choice for the mission [to] Canada (along with his cousin John, a Jesuit priest and the most prominent Catholic in America). Probably the wealthiest man to sign the Declaration of Independence, and certainly the only Catholic, Carroll was the last signatory to die, aged 95. (Independence National Historical Park)

View of Quebec from Point Lévis, by James Peachey c.1784. This image and the next provide a "gunner's eye" view of the city from sites reasonably close to where batteries were established by Arnold during the spring of 1776. During the siege, the pavements were dug up, so that shells would bury themselves in the ground, reducing their effect when they burst. The severity of the weather led to a serious shortage of fuel and, as in Boston, many wooden buildings outside the walls were torn down for firewood. (National Archives Canada – C-013697)

it suited them. Ignoring the latter, he had concentrated on winning the support of the former. Unfortunately, David Wooster had not, and the return of the vengeful Thomas Walker saw American policy depart rapidly from the "brotherly affection" and respect for personal property promised in the letter from Washington that Wooster had distributed on his arrival.

Despite advice to leave the Catholic Church well alone, Wooster insisted on closing the "Mass houses" on Christmas Eve. On the news of Montgomery's death, he took 12 hostages from among known loyalists. He later released them, but leaked a list of 64 "suspects" whom he was prepared to have deported to Philadelphia. He later disarmed the pro-British community, taking two new hostages, and set about reconstructing the militia. All officers would surrender the King's commission, new companies would be formed and new officers elected by the rank-and-file, and all ranks would swear allegiance to Congress. When several officers protested that their Royal commissions were precisely the type of personal property that the Americans had promised to respect, they were imprisoned in Fort Chambly.

Relations were further strained by lack of money. Once their gold was exhausted, the Americans resorted to paper money. This the Canadians shunned due to their experiences in the previous war. The Americans eventually turned to outright confiscation of property and forced labor, though often this was a last resort to alleviate shortages likely to cause the troops to mutiny. When Wooster departed for Quebec, his legacy included new taxes (for which, ironically, no Canadian had voted), bankruptcy, and civil unrest. Hazen, who replaced Wooster until Arnold arrived on 19 April, warned Schuyler that the Canadians were no longer friendly, and could rise up at any moment.

In February, Congress had appointed a three-man commission – Benjamin Franklin, Samuel Chase, and Charles Carroll (the latter two from Maryland, the only colony where Catholicism flourished) – to tour Canada to counter the hostility of the Catholic Church and rebuild trust. To assist them Congress also sent a priest, Father John Carroll, and a French printer from Philadelphia, Fleury Mesplet. On 2 April the

commissioners left Philadelphia and reached Montreal on 29 April, to be greeted by carefully selected "representatives" of the citizenry.

Unfortunately, they had arrived too late and, more importantly, had brought no money to alleviate the army's $14,000 debt (which excluded the $20,000 loaned by James Price). Father Carroll found the local clergy convinced that the Quebec Act had given them all they wanted, and agreed that Carleton's liberal policies had inspired loyalty. Mesplet established his press in the Château de Ramezay, but had not published anything when events brought the mission to a premature end. Franklin's health had deteriorated during the long journey and, despite releasing the political prisoners, he could not redress Wooster's blunders. On 11 May, Franklin and Father Carroll left for Philadelphia.

On 5 May, Samuel Chase and Charles Carroll attended a council of war at Sorel, where all parties agreed that the populous, fertile triangle between Montreal, Chambly, and Sorel must be defended. British reinforcements might soon end the siege of Quebec, but that was no reason to give up the rest of Canada. The commissioners visited Chambly and St Johns and then returned to Montreal to write a report on the state of the defences, before leaving for Philadelphia. The report blamed the short-term enlistments and Wooster's interference for the debacle and demanded his recall. More importantly, Wooster's decision to stop the merchants of Montreal trading with the Indians, in order to restrict the flow of intelligence, was overturned by the commissioners.

The threat from the west

The Americans had deliberately ignored the British posts on the Great Lakes. They did not have the manpower to capture them, but if Quebec fell, those posts would have to surrender anyway. However, in April Arnold sent Captain Timothy Bedel with 400 men and two guns to fortify a trading post at The Cedars, 40 miles (65km) west of Montreal, to prevent trade and guard against a surprise attack.

View of the city and basin of Quebec, by James Peachey c.1781. Quebec was divided into an upper and lower town, separated by a stockade. There were two gates – one, for carriages, ran up a winding road the other, for pedestrians, led to a steep stairway cut into the rock. The city had several churches, but only two taverns one in the upper town, one in the lower. (National Archives of Canada – C-002030)

Captain George Forster, commander of the light company of the 8th Foot based at Oswegatchie, had maintained clandestine links with Montreal and knew of Bedel's mission. The winter had seen the usual Indian migration to his post for handouts, but the warriors had remained longer than usual anticipating action. With 40 Regulars, a dozen British and Canadian volunteers, and 200 warriors under Lorimier, Forster decided to attack Montreal. Leaving on 12 May, he halted at the western shore of Lake Francis, where he learned of Bedel's strength, which demoralized the Indians until a letter arrived from Carleton stating that reinforcements were arriving at Quebec. On 18 May, Forster crossed the lake, headed for The Cedars, and surrounded the stockade.

When Bedel learned of Forster's approach he promptly fell ill, turned over command to Major Isaac Butterfield and fled to Montreal. Lacking artillery, Forster's troops resorted to long-range sniping with the Americans replying in kind. Whilst the firing produced no casualties, the whoops of the warriors created panic inside the stockade. Butterfield was extremely receptive to a summons to surrender, negotiations stalling only when Butterfield insisted that his men retain their arms. As more Canadians arrived to reinforce Forster, Lorimier proposed a simultaneous assault from two sides.

Meanwhile, Arnold had sent Major Henry Sherburn and a further 150 men to reinforce Butterfield and began raising more troops with the intention of following. Sherburn disembarked about nine miles (14km) downstream from The Cedars on the day Forster landed. News of his approach caused Forster to postpone the attack and send some men to watch Sherburn. At this point, Butterfield – unaware that relief was near – offered to surrender if Forster protected his command from the Indians. Forster agreed and the Americans marched out to allow the warriors to plunder the fort. When they had finished, Butterfield and his men returned to their barracks.

Meanwhile, Sherburn had sent a man ahead to learn what was happening at the fort. The man returned with news that Forster was marching to attack Sherburn with over 500 men. Not knowing that this was an exaggeration, Sherburn re-embarked his men, but found out the next day that Butterfield was still holding out, and set off again for The Cedars.

ew of Trois Rivières, by James
eachey c.1784. Founded in
618 at the junction of the
Lawrence and St Maurice
vers, the name derived from an
land that gave the impression
three rivers converging.
itially the second city of New
ance, it lost prominence when
e fur trade moved west, and by
e 1770s its importance was
imarily as a stopover between
ontreal and Quebec. In 1776,
had seven churches, two
nvents, 250 dwellings, and a
pulation of 1,200. (National
chives of Canada – C-002006)

Again, however, his approach was discovered and about four miles (6km) from The Cedars he was attacked by Lorimier's men. Believing himself outnumbered, Sherburn surrendered with 97 of his men. Casualties had been light on both sides, but unfortunately the one death on the British side was a Seneca war chief, whose demise caused the tribesmen to threaten their prisoners.[7]

Having captured Butterfield's and Sherburn's commands (487 men in all) Forster placed the officers in the custody of some priests and set out for Montreal Island with 500 men and the rest of the prisoners. On 24 May, he arrived at Pointe Claire, 18 miles (29km) from Montreal, and learned that Arnold was entrenched around a large stone house at Lachine, with 600 men and some artillery. In fact, Arnold was also expecting the 1st Pennsylvania Battalion and some other detachments, which would eventually give him 1,500 men. Whilst his force grew, Forster's shrank as the independent-minded tribesmen returned home with their plunder. With no further news from Carleton, Forster decided to pull back to The Cedars, but was embarrassed by the numbers of prisoners and decided to effect an exchange. He found Sherburn and Butterfield so eager to remove their men from the clutches of the Indians that not only did they agree to leave four captains as hostages and that no prisoner would serve again during the war, but also that no similar condition would apply to the British prisoners.

As Forster pulled back, Arnold moved up to the eastern end of Montreal Island and on 26 May arrived at Vaudreuil by bateaux. Seeing Forster's men drawn up for battle, Arnold kept out of range of the two cannon Forster had captured at The Cedars. Landing on the opposite bank, Arnold formulated a plan to cross the river at night and attack Forster's flank and rear at dawn. However, his officers – especially Hazen – felt that the Indians would prevent any surprise and that a night march would end in confusion. The acrimonious discussions ended just after midnight and at 2.00am Sherburn arrived under a flag of truce and outlined the response to Arnold's threat to kill any Indian he caught serving with Forster and burn their villages. Arnold knew that any prisoner in their hands would be tortured and killed and agreed to the terms negotiated with Forster (except for the condition on not serving again during the war). It is worth noting that there was no mention of any ill-treatment of the men held by Forster.

The transfer occurred between 27 and 30 May, after which Forster retired to Oswegatchie and de Haas (who had taken over from Arnold) withdrew to Lachine. De Haas ignored an order from Arnold to burn the village of Conosadaga, believing that it would serve no purpose and might unleash forces that he had insufficient force to confront, let alone control. As the prisoners returned south, Congress condemned the actions of Butterfield and Arnold. Using the alleged atrocities as an excuse, they repudiated the agreement, despite written confirmation by one of the four hostages that the allegations of brutality were untrue.

The threat from the east

Forster had achieved only local success, largely because Carleton had not moved from Quebec. With the Americans gone, Carleton had turned his attention to internal security, forbidding those who had collaborated from entering Quebec without written permits. A commission toured the

Major General John Thomas 1724–76, by Benjamin Blyth. Thomas was from Plymouth, Massachusetts and had served with some distinction in the French and Indian War. In 1775 he was one of the first eight brigadier generals appointed to the Continental Army. Promoted to major general after the British evacuated Boston, he took over the Northern Army at Quebec on 1 May and supervised the withdrawal. He was respected by officers and men alike, and his judgment, prudence, and firmness impressed Washington who regarded his death as a serious loss. (Massachusetts Historical Society)

Colonel John Philip de Haas 1735–86, artist unknown. In 1775 de Haas raised a militia company and in October was made colonel the 1st Pennsylvania Battalion. He performed solidly in Canada and apparently saved Arnold from capture during the action at Lachine. (Historical Society of Pennsylvania)

Colonel Arthur St Clair, 1737–1818, by C.W. Peale. St Clair was born in Scotland, joined the Army in 1757, and fought at Louisburg and Quebec. In 1762, he emigrated to America and settled in western Pennsylvania, where he later became a colonel of militia. In 1776, he took command of the 2nd Pennsylvania Battalion and joined the Northern Army. (Independence National Historical Park)

country around Trois Rivières, mobilising the militia, identifying those areas that had been least loyal, and focusing on the desire of most *habitants* to remain neutral. At the same time, Carleton went out of his way to behave humanely to his prisoners. The militia was ordered to search for stragglers, sick, and non-walking wounded who might either starve to death or suffer abuse from enraged *habitants*. Morgan and the other officers captured at Quebec were paroled, each receiving gold and a new shirt as he left for home.

Others, such as MacLean, believed that softness and delay would allow the enemy to recover. Apart from the recapture of the *Gaspé* by the Royal Navy, and the arrival of the 29th and 47th Foot at Trois Rivières, there was no offensive movement. Even when Carleton learned of Forster's victory at The Cedars, rather than head west, he returned to Quebec to greet Burgoyne, who had arrived on 1 June. However, Carleton's absence did leave MacLean in command at Trois Rivières and the active Scot landed the troops and set up camp to await his superior's return.

Meanwhile, at Sorel, MajGen John Thomas had regrouped and met with the commissioners. However, on 21 May, he contracted smallpox and died on 2 June. The previous day, MajGen John Sullivan had arrived with over 5,000 reinforcements and now found himself in command. The commissioners, believing rumors that Carleton's reinforcements were just two regiments from Halifax, urged him to order the army back to Deschambault. Apart from a few zealots, such as Duggan, and the Canadians, the order was not well received until a report came in that MacLean, at Trois Rivières, had only 300 men.[8]

On the afternoon of 6 June Sullivan sent Brigadier General William Thompson with 2,000 men, to investigate Trois Rivières and attack MacLean if circumstances appeared favorable. The troops left Sorel by boat and landed opposite Nicolet. They crossed the river the following night and landed at Pointe du Lac, about seven miles (11km) west of Trois Rivières, at 2.00am. Leaving 250 men to guard the boats, Thompson divided his troops into four regimental columns and a small reserve, and set out through the woods keeping out of sight of the river. Unfortunately, his guide, a local farmer, lost his way (deliberately or accidentally) and led the Americans into a swamp. Struggling out of the woods, Thompson's column found the *Martin* and several other vessels with their guns trained on the road and quickly fell back under a hail of grapeshot.

Meanwhile, the other columns had made better progress. Wayne's column emerged first, and drove back some light infantry and Indians. In the distance across a meadow he saw the church and monastery, but also Fraser's brigade maneuvering into line. As the other columns emerged there were increasingly heavy exchanges of musketry, until Fraser brought up two 6-pdrs rapidly unloaded from one of the transports. He swept the woods with canister at which the entire American brigade broke, pursued by the flank companies of the 9th, 20th, and 62nd Foot. Thompson tried to rally as many men as he could, but only 50 stood with him and he was quickly overrun.

With Thompson and Irvine captured and St Clair wounded, command fell on Wayne. Although it was his first time under fire, Wayne kept his head. He formed a rearguard of 800 men from various units and planned a charge into the town. The British anticipated the move and some Regulars marched out to meet him, until halted by the fire of

Irvine's riflemen. Wayne's men then came under fire from artillery in the defenses around the town and the vessels in the St Lawrence. Realizing that the planned assault was not feasible, he fell back into the woods and ordered one company after another to slip away, finally leaving 20 riflemen to cover the withdrawal.

The Americans lost about 30 dead, as many wounded (including St Clair and Wayne) and over 200 prisoners, including Thompson, his second-in-command William Irvine, and 16 other officers. The survivors sought refuge in the woods – unwisely as it transpired, being plagued by "Musketoes of a Monsterous size and innumerable numbers" all the way back to Sorel. British casualties were eight dead and nine wounded. Men drifted back to Sorel for four days, but in all, about one third of Thompson's command was lost from combat, disease, or desertion.

When Carleton arrived later that day, he immediately recalled a detachment Fraser had sent to pursue the survivors and kept the remainder of Nesbitt's men aboard their transports. Arguably, this was understandable: the survivors would demoralize their comrades back at camp, there was the logistical problem of having even more prisoners, and the knowledge that smallpox was rife among the Americans. Yet his subordinates saw this restraining hand as another example of an overly cautious approach to a numerically weaker enemy and softness toward traitors. On 9 June, Fraser was allowed to take 1,200 men along the north bank of the St Lawrence, while the remaining troops boarded the transports. Even then, it was 14 June before either group moved on Sorel. That evening, the flank companies landed to find that the enemy had abandoned Sorel only that morning.

Initially, Sullivan had intended to fight (he still had 2,500 effectives plus detachments at Montreal, Berthier, Chambly and St Johns), but sickness and defeat had crippled morale. Desertion was now increasing and news that Carleton was approaching led several officers to recommend a withdrawal down the Richelieu. On the morning of 14 June, the baggage and all the artillery light enough to be transported across the rapids were placed on the remaining boats. Evening on 15 June saw the troops camping in the rain at Chambly, except for the Berthier garrison, which had been cut off and had joined Arnold at Montreal.

Arriving at Sorel, Carleton divided his force, sending Burgoyne after Sullivan (now a full day's march ahead) and taking the rest to Montreal in the hope of surprising Arnold. Concerned at the lack of communication with Sullivan, Arnold had sent his aide, Captain James Wilkinson, to find him. Traveling by canoe, Wilkinson saw Carleton's fleet becalmed in the St Lawrence and had galloped back to Montreal on a stolen horse. Within four hours Arnold had evacuated the city. As they left, his men started fires but the militia managed to extinguish them and patrolled the streets until Carleton arrived on 17 June. Taking the road to St Johns, Arnold sent Wilkinson to ask Sullivan for reinforcements, lest the British overtake him.

Wilkinson reached the Richelieu to find Sullivan's men scattered in disorder. Many were asleep, while the commander of the rearguard, Baron de Woedtke, was drunk. Wilkinson found Wayne willing to help, but by the time his troops were mustered Arnold was already safe, having burned several bridges behind him. Sullivan's army left Chambly on 16 June, burning the fort and sawmills, and any boats that could not be used. The following day, he and Arnold met at St Johns; there they decided to

Colonel Anthony Wayne, 1745–96, by C.W. Peale. Educated in Philadelphia, Wayne became a member of the Pennsylvania Legislature and was appointed colonel of the 4th Pennsylvania Battalion in January 1776. (Independence National Historical Park)

Colonel William Irvine 1741–1804, by James Lambdin. Irvine was born in Ireland and served in the Royal Navy during the French and Indian War. He then settled in Pennsylvania and became a member of its Provincial Congress in 1774. As colonel of the 6th Pennsylvania Battalion, he joined the Northern Army, but was captured at Trois Rivières. (Historical Society of Pennsylvania)

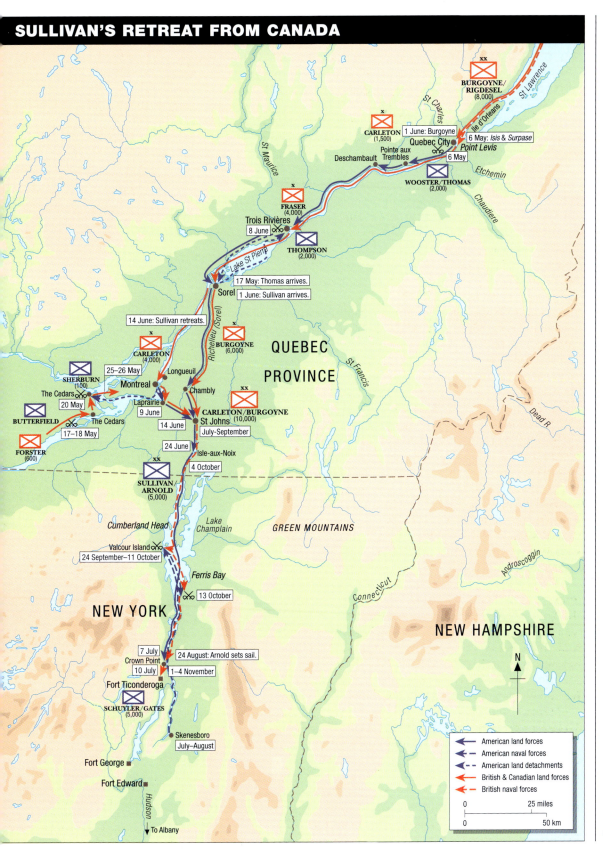

BURGOYNE/ RIGDESEL (8,000)

CARLETON (1,500)

1 June: Burgoyne

6 May: *Isis & Surpase*

Quebec City

Point Levis

6 May

Pointe aux Trembles

Deschambault

WOOSTER/THOMAS (2,000)

FRASER (4,000)

Trois Rivières

8 June

THOMPSON (2,000)

Lake St Pierre

17 May: Thomas arrives.

1 June: Sullivan arrives.

Sorel

14 June: Sullivan retreats.

BURGOYNE (6,000)

QUEBEC PROVINCE

CARLETON (4,000)

25–26 May

Longueuil

SHERBURN (100)

The Cedars

20 May

Montreal

Chambly

BUTTERFIELD

The Cedars

Laprairie

9 June

CARLETON/BURGOYNE (10,000)

17–18 May

14 June

St Johns

FORSTER (600)

July-September

24 June

Isle-aux-Noix

SULLIVAN ARNOLD (5,000)

4 October

Cumberland Head

Lake Champlain

GREEN MOUNTAINS

Valcour Island

24 September–11 October

Ferris Bay

13 October

NEW YORK

NEW HAMPSHIRE

N

7 July

24 August: Arnold sets sail.

Crown Point

10 July

1–4 November

Fort Ticonderoga

SCHUYLER/GATES (5,000)

Skenesboro

July–August

Fort George

Fort Edward

Hudson

To Albany

→ American land forces
⇢ American naval forces
◁-- American land detachments
→ British & Canadian land forces
⇢ British naval forces

0   25 miles
0   50 km

continue the retreat to Crown Point. The dead were thrown into pits, the wounded and sick transferred to the boats, and the army moved off once more.

Burgoyne, having eroded most of Sullivan's 24-hour head start, missed him at St Johns by just two hours (in any event, he had orders not to attack until reinforced by Carleton). Lorimier, who had followed Arnold from Montreal with 100 warriors, tried to ambush the boats at a narrow point in the Richelieu between St Johns and Ile-aux-Noix, but also arrived moments too late.

Typically, Arnold had the last word. He and Wilkinson rode to Chambly to discover Burgoyne's whereabouts. Sighting red coats, they galloped back to St Johns to find one boat remaining. Arnold shot his own horse, ordered Wilkinson to do the same, and then insisted on pushing the boat away from the shore himself, ensuring that he was last to leave Canada.

---

7 Exactly what happened after Sherburn surrendered is unclear, but no report by anyone present mentions the atrocities subsequently alleged. According to one account, a wounded officer – Captain John McKinstry – was to be roasted alive, but was rescued by Brant (possibly recognizing him as a fellow Mason) and the two subsequently became lifelong friends. However, other accounts suggest that Brant was not actually present.

8 MacLean had been reinforced by four battalions under Brigadier General Simon Fraser – the grenadiers and light infantry of the British regiments, along with the 24th and 29th Foot – who were greeted by a three-volley feu-de-joie and shouts of "Vive le Roi!" from the local militia. They were closely followed by three more regiments – the 9th, 31st, and 47th Foot – under Lieutenant Colonel William Nesbitt (who remained aboard their transports) and the sloop *Martin*.

THE BATTLE
ON THE LAKE

Building the fleets

Having expelled the Americans from Canada, Carleton now needed to prevent them from returning. To do that he had to recapture Crown Point and Ticonderoga. However, he knew that he could not do this by land – he also had to control Lake Champlain. He had foreseen this problem even while planning the defense of Quebec. When his senior naval officer, Lieutenant Thomas Pringle, returned to Great Britain in November 1775, Carleton asked him to have the Admiralty supply a large number of flat-bottomed boats for transporting troops and prefabricated parts for larger vessels – ships that could command the lake.

When only 12 gunboat "kits" arrived the following spring, Carleton realized he would have to build his own fleet and placed the dynamic Major-General William Phillips in charge of the project. Aided by a group of naval officers who would all rise to high rank – Lieutenants Charles Douglas, James Dacres, and John Schanck[9] – Phillips made St Johns a hive of activity during the summer of 1776. Unfortunately, the need to manufacture so many smaller boats, and to break down the larger vessels on the St Lawrence in order to get them past the rapids at Chambly, took all of that summer. In September, Carleton informed Germain that he would be unable to advance far enough south before winter set in to assist Major-General Sir William Howe's campaign on the lower Hudson, although he was confident of preventing Schuyler from reinforcing Washington.

Blockhouse and sawmills at Skenesboro. In 1775, Philip Skene was governor of Crown Point and Ticonderoga and owned 60,000 acres at the southern end of Lake Champlain that included iron foundries and sawmills. In the summer of 1776, the Americans added a shipyard where they built the vessels that fought at Valcour Island. (Private collection)

There were no aggressive movements during July and August 1776, although both armies sent out frequent patrols to gather intelligence or catch deserters. On 2 July, a British party attacked Ile La Motte. Others went farther south – on 29 July, the Sieur de Boucherville reconnoitered Crown Point. The presence of over 600 Indians meant that American patrolling was more limited. The most notable incident was the ambush of Lieutenant-Colonel Patrick Gordon by the scout Benjamin Whitcomb. The act incensed the British (and some Americans) and Carleton put a price on Whitcomb's head.

Carleton now had 12,000 Regulars and German Auxiliaries, of whom 4,000 were in garrison and the rest at the north end of Lake Champlain. Burgoyne now occupied the fortified Ile-aux-Noix with six regiments (9th, 21st, 31st, and 47th Foot, von Riedesel and Erbprinz), whilst Fraser was five miles (8km) north of the Quebec–New York frontier with the amalgamated grenadiers and light infantry, and his own regiment, the 24th Foot. In addition, there were five regiments and some artillery at St Johns and Chambly, and more troops at Montreal.

On the American side, Gates had been appointed to lead the army in Canada, which upset both Sullivan – who promptly resigned and stormed off to Philadelphia to complain in person – and Schuyler. Eventually, a compromise was agreed: Gates would command at Ticonderoga, and Schuyler at Albany. On 7 July, after a conference with Schuyler and Arnold, Gates decided to pull back to Ticonderoga, leaving just 300 men at Crown Point. Reinforcements were finally coming in, including New England militia, several much-needed artillery companies and some Stockbridge warriors. By late July there were 7,000 troops at Ticonderoga and another 3,000 defending the Mohawk Valley.

Gates and Schuyler had also agreed a naval strategy. Schuyler nominated Major William Douglass of Connecticut as commodore of the lake squadron, and a friend, Jacobus Wynkoop, as second-in-command. Douglass dithered, hoping for something better, and eventually the New York Provincial Congress gave the post to Wynkoop. His command comprised the *Liberty*, *Enterprise*, and *Royal Savage*, plus the timbers of a partially constructed cutter liberated from St Johns (later named *Lee*).

Since July 1775, the shipyard at Skenesboro had been manufacturing bateaux to ferry men and supplies into Canada, but nothing bigger. Neither Schuyler nor Congress had considered the need for larger vessels until January 1776, whereupon Congress had ordered Schuyler to build a fleet for the lake – whilst at the same time building a wagon road to Fort Edward and a lock at Skenesboro itself. Without experienced shipwrights[10] and sailors, he decided to build "gundalows" (or gondolas) and galleys, which were easy to construct and (relatively) easy to sail. Wynkoop recruited a few experienced sailors from crews working on the Hudson, but he was no ship builder, and certainly no naval commander. In mid-July, Gates brought Arnold (now a brigadier general) back from Crown Point to supervise the work[11] and raise and train crews.

Arnold's first call for volunteers produced just 70 men – insufficient to man one galley – despite the fact that many of the New Englanders had experience of the sea; quite possibly they knew only too well what they were up against. Attempts to recruit men from the coast also failed. Those eager for action were too busy enjoying rich pickings from capturing unarmed merchantmen and there would be none of those on Lake

Commodore Thomas Pringle RN, by Gilbert Stuart. Pringle (often wrongly listed as a captain on 11 October) was a Scot and the senior Royal Navy officer in Canada in 1775. His poor image among historians is not entirely deserved, although he did fail to employ scouting boats that could have spotted Arnold's force sooner, and was undoubtedly culpable in the latter's escape. However, he was trusted by Carleton and after the battle was given the honor of carrying the Governor's dispatches back to London, where he was promoted to post-captain. Pringle showed competence in later years, handling a mutiny with discretion, and ending his career as a Vice Admiral. (National Maritime Museum – PAD3064)

RIGHT **Line plan of the cutter *Lee*. Arnold's fleet was painted red (the same color as local barns). His fleet was manned by 800 men – including those serving as marines – and the combined broadside of the 15 vessels present was about 600lbs (272kg). There were just three 18-pdrs and 12 12-pdrs; the two largest enemy ships alone carried six 24-pdrs and 24 12-pdrs. (National Maritime Museum)**

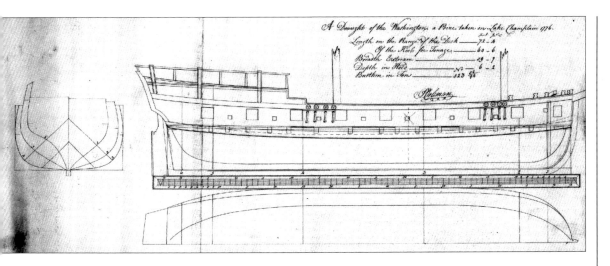

A Draught of the Washington a Prize taken on Lake Champlain 1776.

Length on the Range of the Deck ———— 72-4
Of the Keel for Tonnage ———— 60-6
Breadth Extream ———— 19-7
Depth in Hold ———— 6-2
Burthen in Tons ———— 123 ¾

Line plan of the row galley *Washington*, one of the two largest ships in Arnold's fleet. All of his vessels were built of green wood, which meant that they would not last very long – although longevity was hardly the most pressing issue. Ropes, sails, cannon, and other fittings were found by Schuyler's secretary, Captain Richard Varick, who did as much as anyone to ensure that the fleet was ready in time. (National Maritime Museum)

Champlain. Eventually, 300 draftees, mainly from two New Hampshire regiments, were found to augment the volunteers. Many were the type of men that their commanding officers were glad to be rid of, as Arnold described his sailors and marines as "the refuse of every regiment." Shortages of time and gunpowder would prevent him from making them much better.

In early August the three existing vessels and four new "gundalows" arrived at Crown Point, and on 7 August, Gates ordered Arnold there to take command. Wynkoop took great exception – on one occasion actually firing across the bows of two vessels carrying out Arnold's orders; Gates had Wynkoop arrested, but Schuyler intervened and gave him a shore job, leaving Arnold undisputed commander of the fleet.

By 24 August, Arnold had ten vessels[12] at Crown Point. He took them to the Richelieu to find the enemy, and on 3 September, reports reached

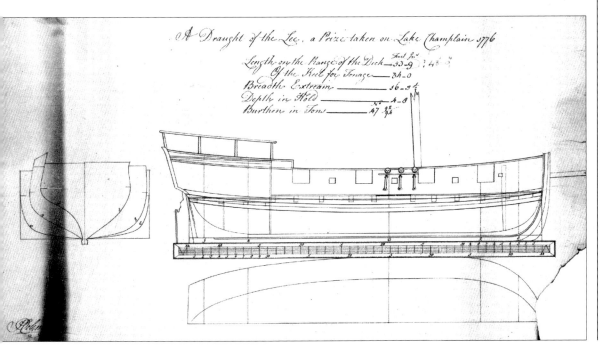

A Draught of the Lee, a Prize taken on Lake Champlain 1776

Length on the Range of the Deck ———— 53-9
Of the Keel for Tonage ———— 34-0
Breadth Extream ———— 16-9¼
Depth in Hold ———— 4-8
Burthen in Tons ———— 47 ¾

Burgoyne that enemy vessels were in the area of Pointe au Fer (Windmill Point). Three days later, after Arnold had been joined by two more vessels, a British patrol ambushed a landing party from *Enterprise* causing several casualties. The return fire from *Enterprise* failed to trouble the enemy but alarmed the 300 Continentals at Crown Point, who prepared for a British attack. On 17 September, two captured British NCOs confirmed rumors of the construction of *Inflexible* and from that point, Arnold decide that his only option was a defensive action in the northern half of the lake. He cruised for several more days, before anchoring between Valcour Island and the New York shore on 23 September.

Carleton, however, did not move until 4 October. General orders for his troops to embark had been issued on 8 September and two days later he had sent his younger brother, Lieutenant-Colonel Thomas Carleton, south with 400 Indians in canoes (followed later by 100 Canadians and 1,200 Germans). But construction of the schooner *Inflexible*, which Carleton considered an essential addition to his force, took four weeks. Like *Carleton*, *Maria*, and *Loyal Convert*, it had been dismantled and ported around the 12 miles (19km) of rapids north of Chambly, to be re-assembled and fitted out at St Johns.

VALCOUR ISLAND

Pringle's squadron[13] – one ship, two schooners, a large "radeau" (or scow), a gondola, over 20 gunboats, and 24 unarmed, flat-bottomed bateaux carrying provisions – finally left St Johns. Without any scouting boats,[14] it moved slowly down the lake looking for Arnold and eventually anchored about 15 miles (24km) north of Valcour Island during the night of 10/11 October. On the morning of 11 October, Pringle set sail again.

At about 8.00am, Pringle's squadron was spotted rounding Cumberland Head by lookouts on *Revenge* (or possibly *Enterprise*, accounts vary). Arnold had transferred his flag from *Royal Savage* to *Congress* and reorganized his flotilla into three divisions, commanded by himself, Brigadier General David Waterbury in the other row galley, *Washington*, and Colonel Edward Wigglesworth in *Trumbull*. Informed of the British presence, he realized that they had not seen *Revenge* and were still heading south. He overruled a suggestion by Waterbury that the flotilla conduct a fighting withdrawal down the lake. Instead, he ordered *Revenge* to sail toward the British until seen and then return, while his four fastest vessels – *Royal Savage*, *Congress*, *Trumbull*, and *Washington* – would sally forth and attack the smaller gunboats, before drawing the larger enemy ships back into the sound. At the same time, the other vessels would form a line of battle across the channel facing south.

However, once he saw the size of the British squadron, he had second thoughts and signaled all vessels to return to the channel, which involved beating back against a head wind (made worse by the high cliffs and trees along the shore). By now it was 10.00am and although the British had spotted *Revenge*, they were now two miles (3.2km) down the lake, and also had to struggle back into the wind. For the gunboats, this involved some hard rowing, but for the sailing ships it was much more difficult, especially as a group, and for the flat-bottomed *Thunderer* it was all but impossible.

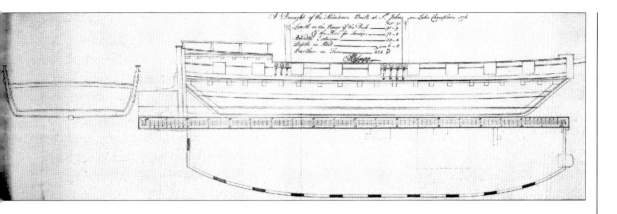

As Arnold withdrew, ***Royal Savage*** ran aground on the south-west tip of Valcour Island after losing its foremast and most of its rigging to several broadsides from *Inflexible*. The vessel was soon surrounded by a swarm of British gunboats and a boarding party from *Loyal Convert* captured 20 men who had failed to escape onto the island, and then turned the guns onto the rest of Arnold's flotilla. A shift in the wind now forced *Loyal Convert* to leeward, abandoning the boarding party (half of whom had by now been killed). With the gunboats unsupported, and under heavy fire from the larger American ships who were using an anchorage on the west side of the island as cover to reload, Pringle ordered a withdrawal.

Around 12.30pm, *Carleton* – commanded by Lieutenant James Dacres – eventually arrived opposite ***Royal Savage***, which had been retaken, and poured in another broadside, before anchoring in an attempt to turn parallel to Arnold's line. However, the swirling wind and a lucky shot, which severed the spring on the cable, turned *Carleton* head on and exposed it to the fire of the entire enemy line for about an hour, during which every officer was wounded except midshipman Edward Pellew. Pellew took command, cut the anchor cable and had some gunboats tow *Carleton*, now with 2ft (0.6m) of water in its hold, out of range.

Aboard the British flagship, *Maria*, Carleton was becoming impatient with Pringle's inaction, especially when a long-range shot narrowly missed the governor and badly wounded his younger brother Thomas.

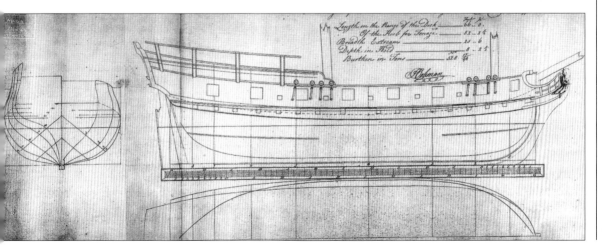

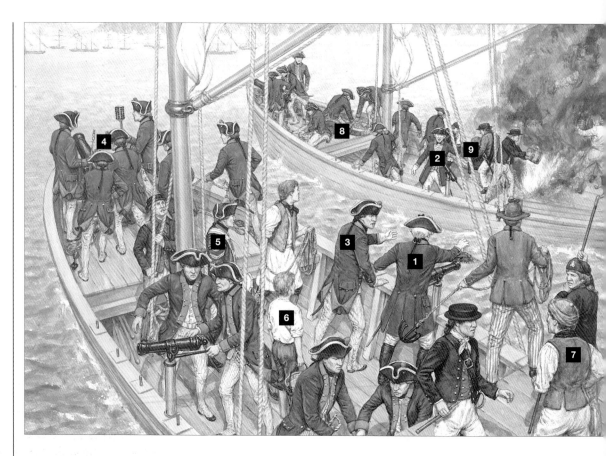

THE HESSE HANAU ARTILLERY IN ACTION AT
VALCOUR ISLAND (pages 79–80)

The squadron commanded by Governor Carleton and Commodore Pringle included a flotilla of gunboats (from 20 to 28, according to various accounts), each armed with a single cannon, ranging in caliber from 6- to 24-pdr. These gunboats were manned by artillerymen, with Royal Navy crews to help sail or row the vessels (which could not sail into the wind, being flat-bottomed). When Arnold's fleet was spotted, on the morning of 11 October, the gunboats formed a line across Valcour Sound, approaching to within 350 yards of the enemy line. From there, they bombarded the Americans, but received a considerable volume of round and case shot (canister) in return, and fell back to a new line some 700 yards from the American squadron. Two gunboats, manned by men of the Hesse Hanau artillery company and commanded by Captain Pausch (1) and Lieutenant Dufais (2), were involved in a serious incident, which is described in Pausch's journal: "Close to one o'clock in the afternoon, this naval battle began to get very serious. Lieut. Dufais came very near perishing with all his men; for a cannon-ball from the enemy's guns going through his powder magazine, it blew up. He kept at a long distance to the right. The sergeant (3), who served the cannon on my batteau, was the first one who saw the explosion, and called my attention to it as I was taking aim

with my cannon. At first, I could not tell what men were on board; but directly, a chest went up into the air, and after the smoke had cleared away, I recognised the men by the cords around their hats [the Hesse gunners wore similar uniforms to their British counterparts]. Dufais' batteau came back burning; and I hurried toward it to save, if possible, the Lieutenant and his men, for, as an additional misfortune, the batteau was full of water. All who could, jumped on board my batteau, which being thus overloaded [Dufais' diligent gunners had also dismounted and carried over their 12-pounder gun!] came near sinking. At this moment, a [British] Lieutenant of artillery by the name of Smith, came with his batteau to the rescue, and took on board the Lieutenant [Dufais], Bombardier Engell, and one cannonier. The remainder of Dufais' men, viz: nine cannoniers and nine sailors remained with me; and these, added to my own force of 10 cannoniers (4), 1 drummer (5), 1 sergeant, 1 boy (6) and 10 sailors (7) – in all 48 persons – came near upsetting my little boat, which was so over-loaded that it could hardly move". Apparently, Dufais' boat had been hit by a round shot that struck the bow end, killing one artilleryman (8) and taking off the leg of one of the sailors (9), then passed through the powder magazine, causing a minor explosion that killed his drummer and the vessel's pilot, and almost destroyed the boat. (Adam Hook)

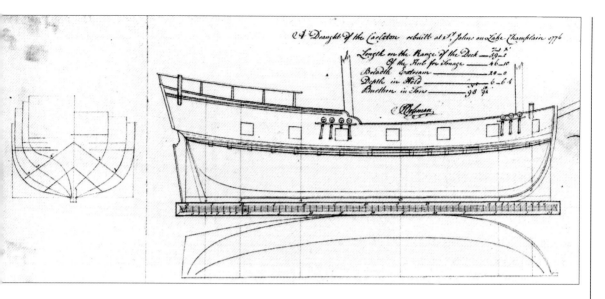

A Draught of the Carleton, rebuilt at St. Johns on Lake Champlain 1776

Length on the Range of the Deck ____ 59-5
Of the Keel for Tonage ____ 46-10
Breadth Extream ____ 20-0
Depth in Hold ____ 6-6-4
Burthen in Tons ____ 58 74

Nevertheless, Pringle remained at anchor and *Maria* was the only vessel – apart from the near-useless *Thunderer* – that did not press on toward Arnold's line.

The battle was now taken up by the British gunboats, which numbered between 15 and 20 (according to Arnold; a German officer estimated 27). As the afternoon progressed, they attempted to close on the Americans, but a hail of grapeshot forced them to maintain a distance of about 700 yards (640m). One boat blew up after being struck by a roundshot that killed one gunner and wounded a sailor. At the same time, two groups of Indians and Canadians had landed on Valcour Island and on the western shore of the lake, and were annoying (but no more than that) Arnold's crews with musket fire.

Around 5.00pm, *Inflexible* finally reached the gunboats and delivered several broadsides, which apparently did considerable damage. The gunboats kept up their firing until dusk (around 5.30pm), by which time most of them had had to be resupplied with ammunition, having used up the 50 round shot each carried. At that point, Pringle ordered all vessels to withdraw and form a semicircle around the southern end of the channel,

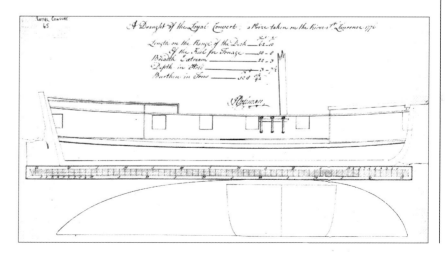

A Draught of the Loyal Convert, a Prize taken on the River St. Lawrence 1776

Length on the Range of the Deck ____ 75-10
Of the Keel for Tonage ____ 50-0
Breadth Extream ____ 20-3
Depth in Hold ____ 8-7½
Burthen in Tons ____ 100 74

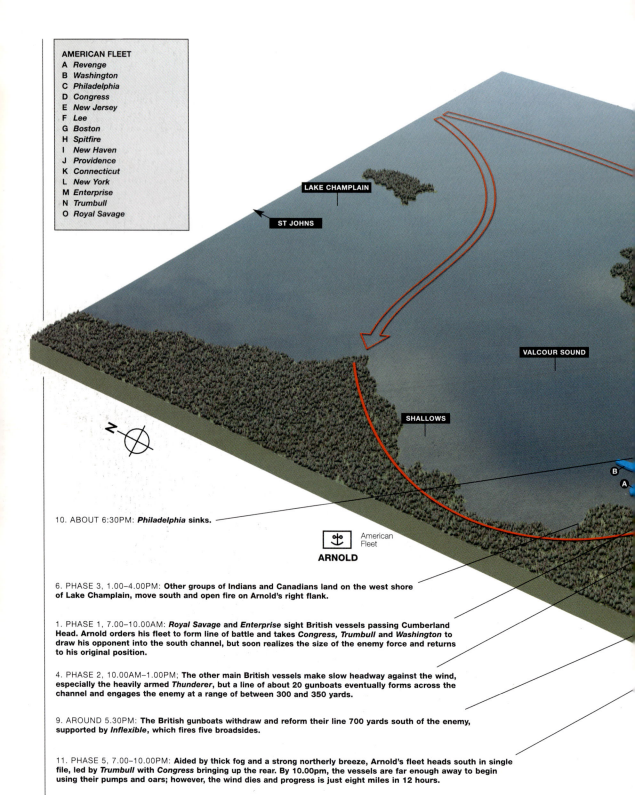

AMERICAN FLEET
A Revenge
B Washington
C Philadelphia
D Congress
E New Jersey
F Lee
G Boston
H Spitfire
I New Haven
J Providence
K Connecticut
L New York
M Enterprise
N Trumbull
O Royal Savage

LAKE CHAMPLAIN

ST JOHNS

VALCOUR SOUND

SHALLOWS

10. ABOUT 6:30PM: *Philadelphia* sinks.

American Fleet

ARNOLD

6. PHASE 3, 1.00–4.00PM: **Other groups of Indians and Canadians land on the west shore of Lake Champlain, move south and open fire on Arnold's right flank.**

1. PHASE 1, 7.00–10.00AM: ***Royal Savage*** **and** ***Enterprise*** **sight British vessels passing Cumberland Head. Arnold orders his fleet to form line of battle and takes** ***Congress, Trumbull*** **and** ***Washington*** **to draw his opponent into the south channel, but soon realizes the size of the enemy force and returns to his original position.**

4. PHASE 2, 10.00AM–1.00PM; **The other main British vessels make slow headway against the wind, especially the heavily armed** ***Thunderer***, **but a line of about 20 gunboats eventually forms across the channel and engages the enemy at a range of between 300 and 350 yards.**

9. AROUND 5.30PM: **The British gunboats withdraw and reform their line 700 yards south of the enemy, supported by** ***Inflexible***, **which fires five broadsides.**

11. PHASE 5, 7.00–10.00PM: **Aided by thick fog and a strong northerly breeze, Arnold's fleet heads south in single file, led by** ***Trumbull*** **with** ***Congress*** **bringing up the rear. By 10.00pm, the vessels are far enough away to begin using their pumps and oars; however, the wind dies and progress is just eight miles in 12 hours.**

THE BATTLE OF VALCOUR ISLAND
11 October 1776, 7.00am–10.00pm, viewed from the south-west showing the bloody exchanges as the British attempt to overwhelm Benedict Arnold's fledgling fleet.

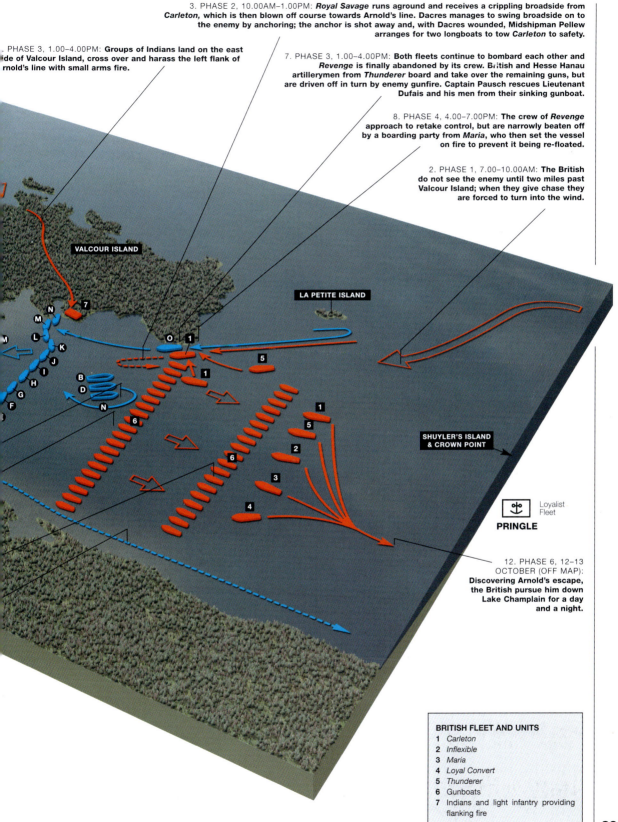

3. PHASE 2, 10.00AM–1.00PM: *Royal Savage* runs aground and receives a crippling broadside from *Carleton,* which is then blown off course towards Arnold's line. Dacres manages to swing broadside on to the enemy by anchoring; the anchor is shot away and, with Dacres wounded, Midshipman Pellew arranges for two longboats to tow *Carleton* to safety.

. PHASE 3, 1.00–4.00PM: **Groups of Indians land on the east ide of Valcour Island, cross over and harass the left flank of rnold's line with small arms fire.**

7. PHASE 3, 1.00–4.00PM: Both fleets continue to bombard each other and *Revenge* **is finally abandoned by its crew. British and Hesse Hanau artillerymen from** *Thunderer* **board and take over the remaining guns, but are driven off in turn by enemy gunfire. Captain Pausch rescues Lieutenant Dufais and his men from their sinking gunboat.**

8. PHASE 4, 4.00–7.00PM: The crew of *Revenge* **approach to retake control, but are narrowly beaten off by a boarding party from** *Maria,* **who then set the vessel on fire to prevent it being re-floated.**

2. PHASE 1, 7.00–10.00AM: The British do not see the enemy until two miles past Valcour Island; when they give chase they are forced to turn into the wind.

VALCOUR ISLAND

LA PETITE ISLAND

SHUYLER'S ISLAND & CROWN POINT

Loyalist Fleet

PRINGLE

12. PHASE 6, 12–13 OCTOBER (OFF MAP): Discovering Arnold's escape, the British pursue him down Lake Champlain for a day and a night.

BRITISH FLEET AND UNITS
1 *Carleton*
2 *Inflexible*
3 *Maria*
4 *Loyal Convert*
5 *Thunderer*
6 Gunboats
7 Indians and light infantry providing flanking fire

ready to finish the job off the following morning. Carleton also sent a message to the land forces on Valcour Island to set fire to *Royal Savage*. Soon after dusk, the powder magazine blew up and the remains of the vessel continued to burn through the night.

Back in the sound, Arnold's fleet had taken a pounding. Around 5.30pm the badly damaged gundalow *Philadelphia* sank. *Washington* and *Congress* had both been holed a dozen times, and *Jersey* and *New York* were both badly damaged. In all about 60 men – almost ten percent of his strength – were dead or wounded, including many officers who had been forced to set an example to the inexperienced crews (Arnold had supervised the loading and aiming of every gun aboard *Congress*). *Washington* and *New York* each had only one officer left alive.[15] Although these were light losses for a naval battle of such intensity (British casualties appear to have been about the same), they seemed heavy to the land-lubbers on the American vessels. In addition, Arnold estimated that three-quarters of his ammunition was gone.

At 7.00pm he called a council of war to discuss the next move. It was agreed that the only option was to try to escape. Around 10.00pm the squadron headed south led by *Trumbull*, hugging the shore and guided only by hooded lanterns on the stern of each vessel. Oars were muffled and – worryingly for some – the pumps were not to be used until well clear of the enemy. A dense fog had formed along the western shore and this, together with Pringle's failure to post adequate sentries and the gunboats laying too far offshore, made their task easier – although they passed close enough to the enemy line to hear voices. Once clear, Arnold's men rowed furiously to widen the distance.

At dawn the next day, Pringle discovered that the Americans were gone, and headed south in pursuit. A strong headwind prevented the British from catching their prey, but it also stopped Arnold from increasing his lead. At Schuyler Island, Arnold let his crews have a few hours rest, even though they had only covered eight miles (13km) and still had another 28 (45) to cover to reach Crown Point. A survey of the surviving vessels led to *Providence* being stripped of its guns and stores, and scuttled. *New Jersey*, leaking badly, ran aground, while the crew of *Lee* simply abandoned their vessel for no apparent reason; both were captured the next day.

On 13 October, the wind shifted to northerly and Pringle's large ships quickly overhauled Arnold's remaining vessels off Split Rock around 11.00am. Arnold ordered *Enterprise* (now a hospital ship) to escape to Ticonderoga, while the rest of his flotilla formed line of battle. The damaged *Washington* was lagging and Waterbury asked for permission to

scuttle, which Arnold refused. The vessel was quickly surrounded by *Inflexible, Carleton,* and *Maria* and was forced to surrender around noon. Pringle then turned his attention to *Congress* and as casualties mounted Arnold pulled into Ferris Bay (an anchorage he had used in August) and ordered the vessels set alight with their colors still flying.[16] Sending his marines up a steep bank to form a firing line, he was the last man to disembark. However, the British chose not to pursue and simply stood off and blasted the enemy vessels into matchwood.

Arnold led the 200 or so survivors to Crown Point, where they were met by *Trumbull, Enterprise, Revenge, New York*, and *Liberty*. They burned the remaining buildings and stores, before heading for Ticonderoga. His losses over the three days were 80 dead, 120 captured (many of them wounded) and all but three of his vessels. There appear to have been no further British losses after 11 October.

On 14 October, a group of Indians occupied the blackened ruins of Crown Point, and three days later Fraser's corps took possession of the fort. The British were only 12 miles (19km) from Ticonderoga and in complete control of Lake Champlain. Washington surmised that Carleton might bypass the fort and head straight for Albany; however, this would have been extremely risky and Carleton was not a man to take risks. Arriving on 20 October, just as the first snow was falling, Carleton devoted his time to stockpiling supplies and ensuring that the prisoners captured in the naval actions were well treated before being returned. Gates was so worried at this humane treatment that he sent the men home, rather than allow them to demoralize their comrades.

On 27 October, some gunboats landed troops at Three Mile Point, just above Ticonderoga, but were forced back by several shots from *Trumbull* anchored behind the log boom that now stretched across the lake. Fraser tried to entice Gates out of the fort again, but the latter was not interested and the standoff continued into November. Carleton considered rebuilding Crown Point then changed his mind. On 2 November, Fraser's troops re-embarked and returned to Canada and ten days later the whole army went into winter quarters, much to the disgust of some officers, including Phillips and Fraser. On 31 December, Bishop Briand celebrated Mass in Quebec at which many who had collaborated with the invaders were forced to do public penance. Afterwards, Carleton threw a lavish dinner for 60 guests, and a public ball to commemorate the first anniversary of the repulse of Montgomery's attack.

---

9 Lieutenant David, who commanded the *Inflexible*, had invented a "drop keel" – a forerunner of the modern yatchsman's centerboard – which was rejected by the Admiralty in 1776; had it been adopted, it would have made *Thunderer* considerably more maneuverable into the wind.
10 Congress overcame this shortage by offering workers at Portsmouth, Boston, and other dockyards $35 a month – paid in advance – to serve at Lake Champlain.
11 At the time, Arnold was facing a court-martial on charges – brought by Hazen – of looting Montreal during the retreat from Canada. The charges were eventually dropped, but only after Gates had used his influence to save Arnold.
12 *Royal Savage*, *Revenge*, *Enterprise*, *Boston*, *New Haven*, *Providence*, *New York*, *Connecticut*, *Spitfire*, and *Philadelphia*; the other vessel on the lake was *Liberty* (stripped of its armament and serving as a hospital ship and storehouse for the fleet). On 6 September, Arnold was joined by *Lee* and *New Jersey*, and on 23 September, by *Trumbull*, *Washington*, and *Congress*. Two more "gundalows" – *Gates* and *Success* – were not completed in time to join the squadron.
13 Carleton was present, but was content to be an observer and leave tactical and administrative command in the hands of the Royal Navy.
14 Pringle is often criticized for failing to investigate the channel west of Valcour Island, but the northern entrance was studded with uncharted rocky shoals.
15 Waterbury and Reed, respectively.
16 Stories persisted that Arnold left wounded aboard the vessels in his haste to burn them. Most (if not all) his casualties from 11 October had transferred to *Enterprise* and the bodies seen on deck were probably men killed that day. Three weeks later, British troops found bodies floating in the water and gave them a decent burial.

AFTERMATH

Carleton's "failure"

Arnold was widely (but by no means universally)[17] praised for his action and the loss of the Lake Champlain flotilla justified by Carleton's withdrawal, the delay to the plan to link up with Howe, and the time won to gather an army at Saratoga. Yet all this is highly debatable; whilst Valcour Island was infinitely superior to the open water as a defensive position, the battle itself did not delay Carleton unduly. A more southerly position could have forced the British to move slowly down the lake, searching every bay and inlet. The bottleneck at Crown Point would have been just as good defensively, and would also have allowed the use of shore batteries with guns more powerful than those of either fleet.

Historians have also followed Germain in blaming Carleton for the late start and extended journey of Burgoyne's expedition the following summer. Yet even if Carleton was culpable in waiting another four weeks to complete *Inflexible* (itself arguable, given limited knowledge of Arnold's strength and *Inflexible*'s eventual contribution to victory), failure to retake Ticonderoga and Crown Point probably had little impact on the events of 1777. Burgoyne's defeat owed far more to his own over-confidence, logistical shortages (especially transport) and his decision to build the road from Fort Ann to Fort Edward. In any event, Burgoyne's army would still have had to concentrate from its winter quarters in Canada and travel down Lake Champlain from St Johns, whilst the recapture of the two forts hardly slowed him at all.

Remains of the defenses of Quebec. One of Haldimand's main tasks was to increase the defenses throughout the province. The 1778 invasion scare prompted major improvements to the defenses of Quebec, including substantial earthworks at Cape Diamond, the remains of which can be seen here. (Author's photograph)

Indeed their recapture in July 1777 was easier than it probably would have been in November 1776. Failure would have been far more costly: heavy losses – irreplaceable until May or June, if at all – would have left Burgoyne too weak to invade and might even have encouraged another invasion by the Americans. And success would have left Carleton having to rebuild Ticonderoga (something the Americans, with far more men, had not done by July 1777), find a garrison, and then keep it fed and supplied for over six months in enemy territory. The earlier thaw farther south would also have allowed the Americans to besiege both posts for some time before Carleton could send relief.

Carleton returned to Quebec to resume his political role and make arrangements to prevent another invasion, rooting out collaborators (showing a ruthlessness that contrasted sharply with his treatment of American prisoners), and finding alternatives to relying on the militia. Indeed, the first meeting of the Legislative Council in January 1777 agreed to replace the more liberal British system with that used under the former régime. However, despite Carleton's more generous interpretation, the *corvée* was no more welcome under British rule; when used to support Burgoyne's army that summer, it led to economic hardship and mass desertion.

Canada after 1777

After Saratoga, Canadians once again felt abandoned and defenseless. As a propaganda gesture, Congress allowed the 30 surviving Canadian militia and the dozens of laborers and bateaux men with Burgoyne to go home. In November 1777, Congress considered invading Canada again and voted to go ahead in January 1778.[18] The British could not replace their losses at Saratoga until May 1778 at the earliest, and the alliance with France might provide extra motivation for the *habitants* – even some *seigneurs* – to rise up.

Despite having short-listed several candidates, Congress decided on a ballot to decide the generals for the invasion force: John Stark, hero of Bunker Hill and Bennington, received eight votes; Marquis de La Fayette and Thomas Conway, six each; Alexander McDougall and John Glover, one each.[19] Eventually, La Fayette was chosen to appeal to the French-speaking populace. Washington was opposed to the plan militarily, but accepted the supremacy of Congress and advised La Fayette to take the post. Congress reluctantly agreed to his choice of Baron de Kalb as second-in-command, rather than Conway, and the inclusion of other French officers then serving in the Continental Army (but at their rank in the French Army). However, Congress still insisted on Conway, McDougall, and Stark serving on La Fayette's staff.

When La Fayette reached Albany, he found every resource – men, horses, equipment, and supplies (especially winter clothing) – lacking.[20] Of those units that had fought at Saratoga, only Hazen's regiment remained. The rest now defended Pennsylvania or the Hudson Highlands. He sent Stark to recruit among the New England militia, and Hazen to find supplies, forage, and clothing to support 3,000 men through a Canadian winter.

Hazen knew that the snow-covered roads would be impassable to men on foot, so he also sought wheeled transport. He acquired almost 500 carriages and over 700 sleighs, but found no civilian volunteers to

General George Washington 1732–99, by C.W. Peale. Washington was entirely in favor of an invasion of Canada in the early years of the war. However, the disasters of 1775 and 1776, and the subsequent buildup of British forces and improvements in Canada's defenses, convinced him that there was little likelihood of success in the future. Ever mindful that he commanded only at the pleasure of Congress, he left the final decision to the politicians, but was not slow to advise his *protégé* to abandon the project as administrative difficulties mounted. (Independence National Historical Park)

Major General the Marquis de
La Fayette 1757–1834, by C.W.
Peale. Eager for independent
command and aware of his value
as a Frenchman, La Fayette
seized the chance to lead the
proposed second invasion.
However, it became evident that
others saw the operation either
as a mere sideshow, or else as a
political opportunity, and he
proposed that it be abandoned.
In reality, success would have
left France with a major problem:
it could not reclaim Canada, but
it was equally unwilling to
promote a North American
"superstate" that could
challenge it economically and
politically. (Independence
National Historical Park)

drive them. The lack of supplies and recruits, and news that Carleton was strengthening the defenses all along the invasion route, led even the firebrand Arnold to advise La Fayette to abandon the project. In March, Congress accepted the Frenchman's assessment and ordered the generals to rejoin Washington.

In the spring of 1778, Major-General Frederick Haldimand, a Swiss soldier of fortune and veteran of earlier wars in Canada, arrived to replace Carleton as governor following Carleton's resignation over Burgoyne's appointment to lead the army into New York. More energetic and forceful than Carleton, but equally intelligent and generous, Haldimand strengthened the defenses of Quebec and Montreal, and organized raids around Lake Champlain and the Great Lakes. In 1780, he entered negotiations with Ethan Allen to create a pro-British "state" of Vermont – a move only ended by the defeat at Yorktown.

After 1778, neither side considered any large-scale operations across the Quebec–New York frontier and by 1780, Congress had abandoned the idea of making Canada the 14th colony. While a surprising number of French-speaking Canadians of all ranks still hoped that a French army would liberate them, by 1783, most accepted the inevitability of British rule.[21]

Nevertheless, the draft American peace proposals presented to the British delegates in Paris in 1782 included a demand that Canada be ceded by Great Britain. The British refused – and had France been party to the negotiations (as it should have been under the 1778 treaty), it would probably have blocked the creation of a North American "super-state" for political and economic reasons. With the British conceding all other demands, the Americans did not press the matter and it was omitted from the preliminary treaty signed on 30 November 1782 and ratified the following year, when the British agreed peace terms with France and Spain. At the end of the war, Canada become a haven for more than 50,000 Americans whose descendants – the United Empire Loyalists – saw off a second American invasion in 1812 and created modern Canada.

---

17 A century later, the naval historian Mahan remarked: "never had any force, big or small, lived to better purpose." However, Jefferson criticized Arnold's actions as "fiery, hot, and impetuous, but without discretion" and accused him of failing "to obtain proper intelligence and retire when faced with a superior force" at Valcour.

18 The Franco-American treaty of alliance, signed in February 1778, stipulated that all British territory conquered by American troops would be part of the United States and any French claims on that territory would be renounced permanently.

19 Given the identity of the generals involved, and the absence of prior consultation with Washington, the planned invasion may have been part of the Conway Cabal (a plot whose existence has never been conclusively established, but which allegedly aimed to replace Washington with Gates, thereby returning control of the war to the New England faction).

20 Barely 900 men were present and fit for duty from a projected force of 3,000; many of these, apparently, were boys and old men.

21 Ironically, this may have guaranteed the preservation of their culture and language, which would probably have been diluted within a larger United States.

THE BATTLEFIELDS TODAY

The Canadian campaign was fought over a large area in two countries, but fortunately the US and Canada share the world's longest undefended border, so touring the surviving battlefields is not difficult. Remember that smaller sites may now be privately owned and always confirm opening well in advance, as they vary from season to season and can be affected by restoration work. Also, many North American sites are open on Sunday but closed on Monday.

American sites

The relevant sites in the United States are Fort Ticonderoga, Crown Point and Valcour Island. For Fort Ticonderoga, take I-87 to junction 28, go south on NY-22 and then east on NY-74 at the second intersection. As well as the "French Lines" and the 1777 defenses, the fort includes a museum and living history displays; there is also a boat trip around both shorelines. It is well worth the climb to the top of nearby Mount Defiance, to understand the fort's strategic position, and why it was more vulnerable to attack from the north than from the south.

The display gondola *Philadelphia II*. This recreation shows how crowded – and vulnerable – such vessels were. (Lake Champlain Maritime Museum)

The defenses near the Porte Palais. The view takes in the area occupied in 1775 by the suburb of La Roche, which was completely destroyed in the siege. Although the defenses are 19th century, it is easy to see how vulnerable Arnold's men were as they passed below. (Author's photograph)

Although it is not strictly relevant to this campaign, it is worth visiting the partially restored site at Mount Independence. Leave Fort Ticonderoga by the main exit and follow signs for the ferry (NY-74); on the Vermont side, take VT-74 to its intersection with VT-73, then continue five miles (8km) south-east and, just before the road meets VT-22A, there is a minor road that is signposted. The 400-acre site is about five miles' drive; there is a visitor center and color-coded trails.

Crown Point can be reached from Ticonderoga by heading east on NY-74 to the intersection with NY-22 (9N), then north to NY-17. The site is four miles (6.5km) beyond the village, beside Lake Champlain Bridge. A visitor center explains its history as an important outpost for French, British, and American troops.

From Crown Point, cross Lake Champlain Bridge to Chimney Point, head north on V-17 to Panton, then turn left onto Sutton Bay Road. This leads to Basin Harbor, home of the Lake Champlain Maritime Museum

Lower town, Quebec. Recently reconstructed buildings replicate the architectural style of the 18th century and also provide some idea of the claustrophobic nature of the street fighting on December 31. (Author's photograph)

(LCMM). Of special relevance are the Nautical Archaeology Center, with a special feature on the Valcour Island "battlefield" (where archaeology is ongoing), and the "Key to Liberty" exhibit, which chronicles the life of Arnold's fleet. Other exhibits include a full-size, working replica of a gunboat (the *Philadelphia II*), a history of boat building in the area, and a fully working 18th-century smithy and forge.

To reach Valcour Island from the museum, follow the road to Vergennes, then US-7 toward Burlington. Either cross the lake via the Essex–Charlotte ferry, or continue into Burlington for the Burlington–Port Henry ferry. Once on the New York side, take NY-22 north to Keeseville, then US-9 towards Plattsburg. If the ferries are not running, go back to Crown Point, and then north on NY-22, through Port Henry, Wadhams, and Keeseville – a scenic route following the lake shore most of the way. From the New York shore it is possible to see where, and why, the main incidents in the battle took place.

The remaining American site of relevance is Isle La Motte, opposite Chazy, about ten miles (16km) north of Plattsburg. Take route US-9, rather than I-87, as the former runs closer to Lake Champlain, and (after entering Canada and becoming route 223) links to St-Jean-sur-Richelieu (St Johns) and Chambly.

Canadian sites

About 15 miles (24km) over the border lies Fort Lennox National Historic Park, which includes Ile-aux-Noix. The restored works date from the 1820s and although a road to St Jean later made the fort obsolete, it is still possible to appreciate the strategic value of the island.

Some 15 miles farther north stands St-Jean-sur-Richelieu. The site of the old fort is now the Royal Military College and a World War II museum, but the remains of some earth ramparts are still visible beside the guardhouse at the entrance. As with many of the rivers in this part of North America, the Richelieu was "canalized" in the 19th century, and is now wider and straighter than in 1775.

Farther north again is Fort Chambly National Historic Park. The fort has been comprehensively restored both inside and out, and boasts a living history unit re-creating French infantry of the colonial wars.

Unfortunately, the battlefields in the Montreal area – Sorel, Quinze Chiens, Laprairie, Lachine, and The Cedars – as well as the city walls, have all been built over. In Montreal itself, however, the Château de Ramezay still stands on the Rue Notre Dame, and is now a museum. It is also worth climbing to the top of the mountain to appreciate the view over the surrounding countryside.

From Montreal, it is a 160-mile (258km) drive to Quebec City. Route 138 is preferable to the North Shore Autoroute, as it not only hugs the shoreline, but also goes through Pointe-du-Lac, Trois Rivières, and Deschambault (again, all developed, leaving no trace of their history).

Once in Quebec City, matters improve somewhat; the city's defenses date mainly from the 19th century (the substantial earthworks in front of the Citadel date from the Revolutionary War, but were built by Haldimand). However, it is still possible to trace the main actions of 31 December 1775. To the south of the city, the Rue Champlain hugs the cliffs leading to Cape Diamond, following the route taken by Montgomery's column. Where it merges with the Boulevard Champlain (most of which

Montgomery's route. The base of Cape Diamond; the point where the road disappears around the corner of the cliff is the approximate site of the blockhouse. Judge Henry (an American prisoner in Quebec) described it as being ... *forty or fifty feet [12–15m] square. The logs, neatly hewn, were tightly bound together by dove-tail work. The lower storey contained loopholes for musketry, so narrow that those within could not be harmed by those without. The upper storey had four or more port-holes for cannon of a large calibre. These guns were charged with grape and canister shot, and were pointed with exactness toward the avenue at Cape Diamond. The blockhouse seemed to take up the space between the foot of the hill and the river, leaving only a cartway on each side. The bulwarks of the city came only to the edge of the hill, above that place; hence down the side of the precipice, slantingly to the brink of the river, there was a stockade of strong posts fifteen or twenty feet [4.5–6m] high, knit together by a stout railing at bottom and top with pins. It was asserted that Montgomery sawed four of these posts himself, so as to admit four men abreast to attack the block-house.*
(Author's photograph)

lies on land reclaimed later), there is a plaque on the cliff, marking the spot where Montgomery was killed.

Immediately above, atop Cape Diamond, is the citadel, which dates from the 1820s but which includes earlier features, including the old French powder magazines and the site of Montgomery's grave until 1818 (when his corpse was taken back to New York City). From the citadel, it is possible to walk along the city wall, some three miles (5km) long, and the only intact example of such works north of the Rio Grande. The walls and the gates are mainly 19th century, but the occasional feature pre-dates Wolfe's siege of 1759. In the Parc de l'Artillerie is the restored Redoute Dauphine, where some of Dearborn's men were held prisoner, and a model of the city from around 1800. East of the Porte Palais, the view from the walls shows how vulnerable Arnold's column was as it moved through St Roche. Within the Vieux-Port, the Sault-au-Matelot still exists and many of the buildings have been restored, preserving the claustrophobic atmosphere that Morgan and his men experienced as they were surrounded by Caldwell and Laws.

The Place Royale marks the main area of the Lower Town and has been faithfully restored to its condition prior to the siege of 1759. The Côte de la Notre Dame is the old carriageway into the Upper Town; at the top stand the Musée du Fort, which has a 400-square-foot (37sqm) model of the city c.1750, and the Place d'Armes.

The area outside the walls is primarily devoted to the battles of 1759 and 1760; the Musée du Québec includes a battlefield interpretation center and there are numerous markers and monuments on the Champs de Bataille. However, nothing remains to indicate the positions of the American siege lines that faced the city from December 1775 to April 1776.

FURTHER READING

The titles listed below are those that relate primarily to operations in Canada and New York from May 1775 to November 1776. For a list of general works on the conflict, see Campaign 37 *Boston 1775* and Campaign 47 *Yorktown 1781*; many of the biographies, diaries, and journals cited in Campaign 67 *Saratoga 1777* actually commence in May or June 1776 and so cover this campaign also.

For the commanders:
Allen, E. *The narrative of Ethan Allen*, Ticonderoga, 1930
Callahan, N. *Daniel Morgan: Ranger of the Revolution*, New York, 1961
Everest, A. S. *Moses Hazen and the Canadian Refugees*, Syracuse, 1976;
Reynolds, P. R. *Guy Carleton: A Biography*, Toronto, 1980
Shelton, H. T. *General Richard Montgomery and the American Revolution*, New York 1994

The following titles are all useful sources of information on the armies and navies:
Gardiner, R. (ed.) *Navies and the American Revolution, 1775-1783*, London, 1996
Katcher, P. *The American Provincial Corps* (Osprey Men-at-Arms Series No. 1), Reading, 1973
Mayer, S. L. (ed.) *Navies of the American Revolution*, London, 1975

However, essential to making any sense of the formations and structure of the "Separate Army" is Wright, R. K. *The Continental Army*, Washington D.C., 1989; whilst Bratten, J. R., *The Gondola Philadelphia and the battle for Lake Champlain*, Texas A&M University Press, 2002, provides similar enlightenment on the creation and operation of the Lake Champlain fleets.

On the campaign generally, the most complete – if no longer the most accurate – titles are Smith, J. H. Arnold's *March From Cambridge to Quebec*, New York, 1903, which includes Arnold's journal; and by the same author, *Our Struggle for the Fourteenth Colony*, New York, 1907 (two volumes). Rather easier to find are more recent works, such as Lanctot, G. *Canada and the American Revolution, 1774–1783*, London, 1967; Stanley, G. F. *Canada Invaded*, Toronto, 1973; and Hatch, R. M. *Thrust for Canada: The American attempt on Quebec 1775–1776*, Boston, 1979. Salsig, D. (ed.) *Parole: Quebec; Countersign: Ticonderoga*, London, 1980, provides useful background information via the orderly book of William Maxwell's 2nd New Jersey Regiment. Two older books, Jones, C. H. *Campaign for the conquest of Canada*, Philadelphia, 1882; and Wrong, G. M. *Canada and the American Revolution*, New York, 1935, should be read with caution as they reflect late 19th- and early 20th-century knowledge and bias.

Numerous journals also cover the campaign: Henry, J. J. *An account of Arnold's campaign against Quebec*, New York, 1968; Kirkland, F. R. *Journal of Lewis Beebe*, Philadelphia, 1935; Romaine, L. B. *From Cambridge to Champlain, March to May 1776*, New Bedford, 1957; Senter, I. *Journal of Isaac Senter*, New York, 1969; and Stone, W. L. (ed.) *Journal of Captain Pausch*, New York, 1969; and by the same editor, *Memoirs, Letters and Journals of Major General von Riedesel*, New York, 1969.

Contemporary maps and charts are found in Marshall, W., and Peckham, H. *Campaigns of the American Revolution*, New Jersey, 1976; and Higginbotham, D., and Nebenzahl, K. *Atlas of the American revolution*, New York, 1974.

American strengths and orders-of-battle can be found in Lesser, C. H. *The Sinews of Independence*, Chicago, 1976; and Peckham, H. H. *The toll of Independence*, Chicago, 1976. For the British, the Public Records Office at Kew is the single most important source for this campaign, particularly WO17.

INDEX